The Mixed + Multiracial
Guide to Wellbeing

of related interest

Therapy in Colour
Intersectional, Anti-Racist and Intercultural
Approaches by Therapists of Colour
Edited by Dr Isha Mckenzie-Mavinga, Kris Black,
Karen Carberry and Eugene Ellis
ISBN 978 1 83997 570 7
eISBN 978 1 83997 571 4

The Latinx Guide to Liberation
Healing from Historical, Generational, and Individual Trauma
Vanessa Pezo
ISBN 978 1 80501 021 0
eISBN 978 1 80501 022 7
Audio ISBN 978 1 39982 646 4

The Muslim Guide to Wellbeing
A Faith-Sensitive Guide to Nurturing Personal,
Spiritual and Relationship Growth
Myira Khan
Foreword by Tahirah Yasin
ISBN 978 1 80501 347 1
eISBN 978 1 80501 348 8

Black Again
Losing and Reclaiming My Racial Identity
LaTonya Summers
ISBN 978 1 83997 318 5
eISBN 978 1 83997 319 2
Audio ISBN 978 1 39981 237 5

Roots and Rebellion
Personal Stories of Resisting Racism and Reclaiming Identity
Foreword by Dr Arun Verma
ISBN 978 1 83997 283 6
eISBN 978 1 83997 284 3

Creative Ways to Explore Identity
Work Creatively with Intersectionality within
the Therapeutic Professions
Kristina Stamatiou and Natasha D'Aguiar
ISBN 978 1 83997 894 4
eISBN 978 1 83997 899 9

THE MIXED+ MULTIRACIAL GUIDE TO WELLBEING

Navigating Family, Identity + Healing

NAMALEE BOLLE

Jessica Kingsley Publishers
London and Philadelphia

First published in Great Britain in 2026 by Jessica Kingsley Publishers
An imprint of John Murray Press

2

Copyright © Namalee Bolle 2026

A CIP catalogue record for this title is available from
the British Library and the Library of Congress

ISBN 978 1 80501 365 5
eISBN 978 1 80501 366 2

Printed and bound in the United States by Integrated Books International

Jessica Kingsley Publishers' policy is to use papers that are natural,
renewable and recyclable products and made from wood grown in
sustainable forests. The logging and manufacturing processes are expected
to conform to the environmental regulations of the country of origin.

Jessica Kingsley Publishers
Carmelite House
50 Victoria Embankment
London EC4Y 0DZ

www.jkp.com

John Murray Press
Part of Hodder & Stoughton Ltd
An Hachette Company

The authorised representative in the EEA is Hachette Ireland, 8
Castlecourt Centre, Dublin 15, D15 XTP3, Ireland (email: info@hbgi.ie)

*With heartfelt gratitude to everyone who
has supported me in this book*

In memory of Sara Sharif (11.01.2013–08.08.2023)

Contents

Introduction

Why do mixed people need a guide to our well-being when we have got 'the best of both worlds'?

I remember a time when I would have had this thought... back when the mainstream understanding of mixed and multiracial identity had convinced me that I was simply lucky to be born into this wonderfully multicultural experience – and no more discussion was necessary...

Throughout my life I have got the distinct impression that the complications and difficulties of being mixed – which can accompany the joys – is seen as a taboo subject. It feels like no one wants to unearth the uncomfortable truth of what we can actually go through.

When Meghan Markle married Prince Harry, there were plenty of opinions and talking heads to discuss her experience. But virtually none of these opinions were from *mixed* people or a *mixed* perspective.

More often than not, the challenges that come with being mixed in a monoracial world are completely erased from conversations. I'm pretty certain you will know what the term 'biracial' means. But you might not be so familiar with the lesser known term 'monoracial' – which describes any person of singular race. You will have come across the term 'non-binary' in relation to gender, but might not have considered that mixed people are 'racially non-binary'. Much like gender non-binary people, mixed and multiracial people are *both* (or more) races rather than just one or the other.

Each of us will come to this book with our own story and experiences that led us to picking it up. Because experience is central to the subject of the book, I'm going to start by sharing how I came to write it.

Black Lives Matter happened right in the middle of my clinical training as a psychotherapist in 2020 when I was in my early forties, and I found my calling specialising in cultural issues, race and trauma.

Through co-chairing our students of colour group, I and others in my college spoke out about the systemic racism in the mental health industry, raising questions of how we could better help our clients of colour to be *seen* in all aspects of their identity.

I felt honoured to be able to help advocate for others. I also began to realise that my British-born Sri Lankan and Dutch-Jewish heritage mixed identity was much harder for me to explain. I struggled with elaborating on my own experience of being mixed, in the way I could empathise with the experiences of non-mixed BIPOC (Black, indigenous and people of colour) people.

Eventually, I realised I didn't know where to start with what I had actually been through as a mixed person; I just couldn't connect with my own authentic feelings about how to describe it. Sure, I *knew* I was mixed, and I had even celebrated my multicultural heritage in various creative ways in my life prior to becoming a therapist. But had I *ever* actually been seen as a 'multiracial' person? Had I ever truly *seen myself*? By seeing myself I mean, had I deeply understood my mixedness and what it means to carry multiple races in one human? I have always felt a lot of injustice in the world, but surely none of that was about my own mixed identity... *was it?*

If it was (which felt impossibly weird and even wrong) then how on earth would I ever know how to untangle any of it, or explain it? And when was the right time to speak up about my own multiracial identity? I started to wonder. The harrowing truth is that the answer to that question seemed to be, actually, *never!*

Here are some questions that I found myself grappling with which you may have encountered yourself:

- How do I *really* feel about the term 'mixed race'?
- Do I carry shame about only being 'half'?
- How would I know if other mixed people felt similarly when we are such a racially diverse group?
- How would others even understand what I mean, if I were to speak about it?
- Is this my own fault?
- Do I even have a right to speak on this, with my... (drumroll)... mixed privilege?

As I posed these questions to myself, I started recognising the same impulse in clients, friends and process groups and realised that these internal responses are very common in mixed people. Many of us are often completely unaware of the way that being mixed might impact us as we navigate life in a world that doesn't understand us – and very often *misunderstands* us.

'Intersectionality' is the term for combined identities where race, class, gender, neurodivergence, etc. all overlap at a kind of identity crossroads. It helps us gain a better understanding of a person's entire multidimensional identity. I feel we can do better in recognising how mixed and multiracial identity interlinks with other categories of our intersectionality – and how this aspect affects us in ways that require much deeper exploration individually and as a collective.

Beyond my own personal experience, I've become increasingly aware as a mental health clinician how little the mixed and multi-racial experience is allowed to exist on its own terms. We are already the fastest-growing ethnic demographic in the UK and with a 276% increase in growth in the US from 2010 to 2020, multiracial people are set to become the majority population in America by 2050![1] So, surely it is in everybody's interest to consider how mixed people are treated?

We know that race is a social construction, *not* a biological fact. But race has *become* real because of slavery and colonisation. And mixed and multiracial people are born smack bang right in the middle of these conflicted racial dynamics.

In 2014 the National Children's Bureau reported that 'mixed-race children are "being failed"' in treatment of mental health problems.[2] In 2021, *The Face* magazine, whose audience is young people, ran the headline 'The unspoken mental health burden of being mixed-race', stating that whilst we know about 'the psychological impact of racial trauma, many mixed-race people are still quietly grappling with the impact of growing up between multiple cultures'.[3]

I'm saddened by how little attention and acknowledgement is given to real-life experiences of mixed and multiracial people, no matter where we are in the world. As a therapist I often work with clients who feel something before they actually consciously register it. Likewise, the mixed experience must be emotionally felt by us first before it can be understood.

So, within this book we start to explore the racial identity by jour-neying inwards before we work through to think about the external impacts.

My primary aim in writing this book is to help *you* recognise and become aware of hidden feelings or responses, and to give you the support to feel confident in unpacking them.

How can any of us explain something about ourselves to others if we don't yet fully understand ourselves? Similarly, if we don't feel we have the right to claim our own experiences, how can we practise self-care?

My hope is that this book will help you to connect with how it *feels* to be multiracial. It will help you to understand yourself in relation to the world, and will provide you with language to describe your experience in a way that feels meaningful, and which is not imposed upon you.

You might disagree with some of my ideas in this book – if you do, that's great. My aim is to help you to recognise and articulate your own sense of identity and outlook.

LANGUAGE

Deciding how I should address mixed and multiracial people for this book was a challenge. We all have different ideas about what we like and don't like to be called, and the terminology to describe us is in constant flux – whether 'mixed', 'mixed race', 'mixed/multiheritage', 'biracial', 'dual heritage', etc.

Personally, I'm not a fan of the term 'mixed race'. No other 'race' is expected to say the word 'race' when describing themselves! It makes me feel like I have to point out my deviation from the 'normal' race. It is my hope that the term 'mixed race' will slowly become obsolete – a bit like 'half caste' did. But I'm mindful that mixed people themselves all have varied opinions and I also recognise that mixed race is still widely understood to describe us as well. I respect that some mixed people will say they don't mind the term mixed race... I guess time will tell how we will be described in the future...

I appreciate that until we are a bit further along in history, it is helpful to use 'mixed race' at times for clarity, especially when distinguishing between a racially mixed person rather than a singularly culturally mixed one. So, I have used mixed race a few times in this book, where necessary, but for the most part I will refer to our group mostly as mixed and/or multiracial so as to be clear I am also speaking about racially mixed folk with two or more heritages.

I have also written this book for parents and carers of mixed and multiracial children who are looking for some guidance. If this is you, thank you for picking up this book and caring for your child's identity in this essential way. I know this information is not easy to come across and I hope to provide some answers and suggestions to help you along, or to at least point you in the right direction with information for you and your mixed family.

Other readers I have in mind are those mental health professionals who believe in the importance of recognising, understanding and valuing the mixed and multiracial experience, because your client/patient deserves to be seen clearly in *all* of their identity.

I do also want to acknowledge the often forgotten experience of bi-culturally mixed people who have monoracial parents of the same race but from different cultures/countries, because I know that you will no doubt relate to some of the experiences described in this book too!

Lastly, I write humbly for anyone who loves us! Whether a partner, a trusted friend, a caring parent or relative or simply if you are an admirer of a mixed and multiracial person, then this book is for you to step inside our world and understand better our experiences.

HOW TO READ THIS BOOK

My aim is to take you on a journey of the spectrum of what mixed and multiracial people might encounter, with lots of prompts, self-enquiry, reflections and encouragement of *how* to deal with each challenge and which steps to take.

I have split this book into three sections to make it easier to acknowledge what might come up on each stage as you reveal, identify and transform your mixed experience. There will be times when you may feel some unexpected emotions; in particular hidden grief may emerge as we explore mixed childhood memories or other past experiences that resonate. So, I invite you to take your time with it all and read this book in whichever way works for you personally. Allow yourself the freedom to dive in as you wish, to skip some chapters if you need and then to go back to them when you feel ready.

Like all groups, mixed and multiracial people are not a monolith. Unlike other racial groups we are made up of a vast multitude of ethnicities and all come together in our shared experience of defying race binaries.

Alongside my own voice, I have included as many different stories of people with various racially and culturally mixed backgrounds as I possibly can to illustrate how (although we may differ considerably) mixed people also have a lot of common similarities in our experiences of grappling with monoracial and monocultural rules and regulations.

Part 1

UNPACK

Chapter 1

Living between races is exhausting!

MULTIRACIAL INTERROGATION + HOW IT AFFECTS US

You want to know
if I'm wholesale
if I'm discount
if I'm 100%.
you want to know if I'm qualified
and justified
you want to know
you want to know

'NOT HOMOGENEOUS', DR ISHA MCKENZIE-MAVINGA

'WHAT ARRRE YOU?' people demand as if encountering a strange unknown item, an alien even. They may as well be saying 'what is it??' and pointing at 'IT' with a stick.

The peculiar urgency from others to immediately zone in on my race before anything else about me is the everyday stuff of the mixed and multiracial experience. Yet this line of questioning is very much accepted...

When I was working as a stylist with a white singer in the 2010s, after a couple of days on the shoot she still hadn't learned my name yet, but she felt compelled to shout across the lunch table with a mouthful of sandwich, 'What arrrre you?' in a sing-song tone.

After that, I spent the day on the precipice of tears at how objectified I felt. I had no way of proving anything, but the delivery was such that I knew some form of under-the-radar racism had occurred that I would never be able to claim. It's hard to call out because this kind of thing can appear, and actually often is, quite innocently intended. I don't think people realise that even when we may be playing along, more often than not mixed people are not fans of this invasive questioning and would prefer you take your time and get to know us before honing in on something as personal as our race.

What the singer did wasn't unusual though. You may have noticed it's pretty much unspoken universal knowledge that mixed and multiracial folk are commonly expected to racially self-disclose our mix when a curious stranger has noticed us and asks us to share this intimate information about ourselves. Questions about our race are something we often feel obligated to answer, without considering the intention behind the interaction or even if it feels OK to us. If you have dared question someone's right to ask this when they haven't even asked for your name yet, I'm glad you have some awareness of your human rights.

Have you ever wondered what it is exactly that makes people feel so emboldened to ask for something so personal and so racially invasive from someone they don't even know?

RELENTLESS OTHERING IS *NOT* FUN FOR US!

If you look online you will find hordes of non-mixed people obsessively commenting on viral posts about mixed people's identity and appearance as if it's some kind of sport. From my Sri Lankan and Dutch mixed perspective I have always experienced this rather entitled expectation to just *KNOW what I am* as racially loaded in ways that are quite hard to pin down or describe. It has become an unnameable feeling sitting just underneath my conscious awareness. Often it stays there, in limbo, because this question is usually asked in a way that seems highly positive. 'Oh I LOVE mixed race babies, they are the *best*-looking children!' people will often assert to prove that their line of questioning is completely reasonable and they are just 'overcome' with joy at the sight of a multiracial person. But when monoracial people coo and peer at us as the spectacle, it is often apparent to us that this is actually more dubious than it appears, even when the person asking thinks they are merely being friendly and even when the receiver seems 'grateful' for the 'compliment'. Exotification of 'the other' often happens when there is a dominant racial way of being, like white supremacy, but it also comes from *within* BIPOC communities themselves when we don't fit their visual expectations either.

People might say:

- 'You look so exotic.'
- 'What are you?'
- 'Where are you from' or 'Where are you really from?'
- 'Mixed race people are the BEST-looking.'

Often these types of enquiries are flattering, making it hard to object without sounding ungrateful. Yet I am always left with that icky feeling in my gut that speaks to something deeper in the multiracial collective consciousness. It's hard to explain though, because we haven't had the language to explain why it just feels so *off*.

Lurking in the shadows of US history, mixed and multiracial people were historically shunned; abandoned as children, designated unworthy, shameful and illegal. It wasn't until 1967 when *Loving vs Virginia* overruled the miscegenation law (where interracial marriage and sexual relations were criminalised) that people of different races were finally allowed to legally marry. Things then slowly started to change, although interracial marriage was *still* banned in some American states up until 2000! 'Mulatto', the derogatory term used to describe us, likens a mixed person to a mule: the infertile offspring of a donkey and horse. The word mulatto was still being used to describe us when I was at school and is *still* used to this day in many countries, with many defending its usage.

I was born in Guildford, an affluent suburban town in England, barely a decade after the legalisation of so-called 'mulattoes' in America. I really didn't like to be noticed as a young child at all and was seen as 'shy' but I wasn't – I was just terrified of the racism I experienced. I couldn't explain my heightened self-consciousness around my appearance for a lot of my adulthood either, where my white-presenting 'pretty privileged' looks became a 'positive' focus of my existence.

When race was involved for me as a young child, however, it usually meant negative attention. Children made jungle noises at the teacher's mispronunciation of my name when the register was called and used the P-word in the playground. During a project for a school stamp making exercise, we had to get other children to draw around the projection of our head shapes, and my friends made me feel like I was a different species. 'Eww look Namalee's forehead is weeeerirrdd', they pointed out. Looking back it was an early introduction of the race-sciencey remarks that would follow me throughout my early school life. To ask me about my race still often feels indirectly dangerous to me, like if I don't comply with the expectation of what you think I am, if I don't play along, explicit racism will be inevitable.

White people *really* want to know, 'Are you one of us, or one of them?' And people of colour *really* want to know, 'Are you the oppressed or the oppressor?' Unlike white people they are unconsciously trying to gauge how racially *safe* they are around me. This makes me feel both apologetic for existing in the first place, but also angry, because I didn't *choose* to be born 'in between'! I really don't want to cause anyone else anxiety by just being me, but why should me existing exactly as I am be so uncomfortable for others to accept? Others needing to instantly put me in a racial box helps calm their angst about me for being racially unboxable. They will say all kinds of things to extract the information they need from me no matter how invasive, and I've often felt there's a strange subtext at play, where the racial suspicion of me is unnervingly palpable.

I have not until very recently possessed the integration of self to even acknowledge and communicate to outsiders that I am actually allowed to be both sides of myself at once. In the past others have told me I *must* decide, I *must* choose a side, and I used to agree with them. I never knew I had a choice until I read the *Bill of Rights for People of Mixed Heritage* by Dr Maria Primitiva Paz Root, which was published in 1994. As a Filipino American clinical psychologist and educator, Dr Root was the first scholar to speak up for mixed people's rights. Written over 30 years ago this bill is shared widely today on social media and mixed blogs with some saying they have printed it out and stuck it up in their homes to inspire them. Reading it still makes me feel tearful as it *completely* validates all the inexplicable feelings I have silently carried inside me my whole life. It's a sentiment one Reddit user captured in their post about the Bill.

> *I think it encapsulates the essence of our unique experiences. The right not to justify our existence is a powerful statement, as it frees us from the burden of proving ourselves in a world that sometimes expects us to fit neatly into predefined racial categories. We should have the autonomy to self-identify as we see fit, reflecting our complex heritage. Moreover, the right to create a vocabulary to discuss our mixed heritage is crucial, as it empowers us to express our unique experiences. Overall, these rights are not just a set of guidelines; they are a source of pride, allowing us to navigate our diverse world with authenticity and confidence.*[1]

The silent erasure of multiracial people can be observed in the UK Census which only introduced a category for mixed race people as recently as 2001; in the US the Census recorded mixed people in various ways but it was only in 2000 that people were given the option to identify as multiracial by specifying more than one race category.

Mixed expression is not a new concept – in fact slavery-era multiracial poets have reflected on their mixedness in works like W.B. DuBois' *The Quadroon* in 1911, Joseph S. Cotter, Jr's *The Mulatto to His Critics* in 1918, and Georgia Douglas Johnson's *The Octoroon* in 1919. However, if you are wondering why it feels like everyone is talking about being mixed and multiracial all of a sudden, it's likely because the mixed population is growing exponentially for the first time in history and many more of us now feel validated to *claim* our mixedness. Officially owning our 'mixed feelings' wasn't really seen as permissible in the mainstream until 1994 when *The Bill of Rights for People of Mixed Heritage* started to influence a brand new generation!

Mixed and multiracial people from Gen Z born between 1997 and 2012 with access to social media are now coming of age in an era where they have licence to speak with agency about what it's *actually* like to be mixed for the very first time in history on such a grand scale. Tiktokers like @pbandcurls, who explains on her channel how mixed people are 'exiled' from both of their cultures, and @hennygvo, who makes humorous videos expressing his white-presenting Black mixed struggles, are redefining the racial status quo.

OUR MIXED IDENTITY IS DICTATED BY OTHERS

In the identity interrogation process that I've described above, mixed people find ourselves pitted against monoracial societal race rules and regulations, and as a result can be made to feel that it is *our* responsibility as multiracial people to soothe others who are affected by how *we* present. Allowing others to 'solve' us will calm the discomfort that our existence creates for everyone else, because *we* are the problem due to being outsiders of the 'normal' racial system. This places all the burden onto us for looking *racially unexpected*. We become props for other people's fascination and/or fear. They just need to know what the HELL we are as fast as possible!

> *'She's definitely Filipino!'*
> *'Noooo but her features look South Asian.'*
> *'Nooo she looks JUST like my friend who is LATINA!!'*

People claim the right to verbally bat it out of me, until they get the 'right' answer – the answer they think fits me best. If they do get an answer from me which is different to the answer they so desperately want, they might act frustrated or disappointed that I am not what they thought. 'Noooooo you're not Sri Lankan – absolutely NO way!!!' They tyrannically demand and instruct me that I am wrong. That I am essentially asked to partake in my own race science quiz is one thing; it's quite another when they then refuse to believe reality when I tell them the truth about my proud heritage. Like many others I have often second guessed and interrogated myself when this occurs, like 'how can I possibly refuse to answer if everyone is having such a great time demystifying me? Shouldn't I just stop being such a party pooper?' Here are some terms that can help cast some light on what's happening to me here:

Each of us has a **genotype** – the unique sequence of DNA in our cells which is only observable under microscopes! Our **phenotype** is the observable manifestation of this DNA – how it shows through our physical appearance. **Racial phenotypes** are characteristics often used to classify people into racial groups, and might include features like skin tone, hair types, bone structure and facial features. As I've outlined previously, scientists are in agreement that race is a *social* construction, so mixed people's appearance regularly challenges expectations of stereotypical racial phenotypes.

Gaslighting yourself about your multiracial phenotype might sound like:

- 'I'm so lucky to get SO much attention, when so many don't, so I won't speak up that I actually find this upsetting/offensive.'
- 'They don't mean anything by it and I don't want to be rude.'
- 'I have light skin privilege so that means I don't have the right to call this out.'

Sophie Kanno is an activist from South California who runs the Instagram account @MixedPresent:

I've literally said I am Japanese, German, Scottish and Welsh, but still people have been like, 'are you, like, Hawaiian? I think you're Hawaiian'. I had this dude literally argue with me. And he was like, 'No, you're Thai. I'm pretty sure you're Thai.' These are just experiences that we have extremely frequently. So this is something that's constantly on our minds.[2]

Sophie articulates the psychologically draining rigmarole which, until recently, has been such a normalised part of our existences. Many of us will not know any mixed people to talk to about these experiences – to unpack how it makes us feel, what's OK and what's not OK.

You may have experienced 'Where are you from?' or 'Where are you really from?', which most people of colour are asked too. There's a subtext to this question – that you somehow don't belong, whether mixed or not. But 'what are you?' is something a bit different – it's a level of extreme interrogation into our mixedness, because the observer is able to see we are mixed.

Sophie further clarifies this:

Monoracial people are always asking why mixed people are so obsessed with talking about being biracial. The answer is actually really simple. From the time we can converse with anyone, multiple people will come up to you just in your day to day and they need to know what race you are, they need to know why you look like that. It's just presented in your day to day and you're asked 50,000 different ways – 'What are you?'

PINPOINTING MIXED + MULTIRACIAL MICROAGGRESSIONS

Insulting mixed people's appearance is actually just as common as the unhelpful obsession over idealised 'mixed beauty'. When we don't fit mixed stereotypes of how we are *supposed* to look, sometimes there is a kind of disappointment inflicted on us for failing to fulfil monoracial expectations. **Microaggressions** are the types of subtle, complicated, sometimes unintentional but nonetheless offensive remarks directed towards people from marginalised and minoritised groups. Mixed and multiracial microaggressions often merge with standard racist micro-aggressions, but we are targeted a bit differently too, with comments often focused on our 'phenotypical ambiguity' and the way we often don't look racially stereotypical.

The Barbadian and Irish-British comedian Nathan D'Arcy Roberts sums up this dehumanisation when he recounts a real-life encounter by 'joking' in his stand up performance: 'I never get asked where I'm from. I only get asked where are you "FROM from?"'[3] continuing that the woman shouted at him across the street *just* to ask this. He then asks her why she wants to know? Her reply: '*Because I thought you looked WEIRD.*' With that, her curiosity was satiated and she then simply walked away. Cue hysterical audience laughter.

By turning this all into humour, Nathan conveys so well how easily these specific multiracial microaggressions are overlooked. The woman only said 'weird' right? It's not like she called him the N-word – so what's the problem?! Is he even allowed to feel upset about that without being seen as attention seeking and dramatic? The thing is, just because overtly racist language wasn't used, doesn't mean it's not a racist microaggression. The woman didn't have to be explicit because the implication is that he looks *abnormal* in comparison to 'normal race'. Anything where someone is pointing out someone looks defective or wrong in some way feels like racism, because it *is*, even if it's not explicit racism.

The ease in which these ambiguous microaggressions are aimed at us is well documented. In 2016 British singer and artist Charli XCX defended her mixed Indian Scottish heritage after a commenter made a microaggressive remark online saying 'XCX always looks dirty'. Charli screenshotted the comment, responding, 'ugh. wow. just wow'. She then tweeted explaining why the label 'dirty' is offensive, stating, 'i am extremely proud of my indian heritage. i love my roots & my family. don't call me/anyone "dirty" bcoz of the colour of someone's skin.'[4] I imagine the perpetrator did not expect a white-presenting mixed person to speak up at all, let alone as strongly as that, due to the victim's proximity to whiteness. I'm really happy that Charli had the confidence to call out the mixed racism for what it was, but that's not always easy to do. When Meghan Markle was likened to a 'mutt' – a dog of mixed breed – in a British tabloid newspaper famous for its bigotry, no one said a word about it, likely due to it being a racial slur specifically intended for mixed people. A white journalist likening a Black mixed woman to an animal was cleverly worded to mention 'mutt' rather than simply a dog, so it went unnoticed. The racism aimed at mixed people is often complicated and purposely confusing, aimed to strategically gaslight us and create division, with the offenders relying on there being no united group to call it out on our behalf.

PERMISSION TO *OWN* WHAT HAPPENS TO US

So what does all this gaslighting do to the mixed and multiracial sense of self? Years of being expected to laugh such questions and comments off while receiving the messaging that it's not as bad as 'real racism' naturally stores up sadness and resentment. We might find ourselves questioning whether what has happened ever took place at all, due to how easily society dismisses mixed and multiracial experiences. In my therapy sessions with mixed clients, we will often carry out deep investigations into how these kinds of experiences have affected them.

I'm glad Nathan D'Arcy Roberts, in common with many other comedians, uses the art of turning this all into humour. But mixed people know that the joke is really that he cleverly gets the audience to laugh along at his pain, because that's often what happens in real life when we tell the truth of our experiences to anyone. A lot of us do turn to humour to deal with this. Just think – why else are there so many mixed and multiracial comedians talking about being mixed?! If you don't have a network or community to listen and unpack these experiences, you might as well take to the stage and explore it there! More recently I have occasionally taken to comedy as well. It works a treat if I'm being particularly interrogated for being 'exotic'. 'I'm a pineapple' I will reply. Or 'I'm whatever you want me to be' I will say seductively, if I feel like I need to completely derail the conversation so that I can distract them with shock and laughter... and then I can try and escape!

Don't get me wrong, I fully appreciate that *curiosity* about each other, including race, is a natural response upon encountering someone who just simply looks different. Even when people say they have genuine intentions we must remember that racial microaggressions can be both conscious and unconscious, because the effect on the receiver is the same. The truth is we might hesitate to call out this kind of mixed and multiracial microaggression as we may feel confused or worried about upsetting others. But we should keep in mind the impact of these actions upon us, and remind ourselves that it is not OK to cause anyone to feel racially dehumanised.

THE NORMALISATION OF MIXED + MULTIRACIAL INTERROGATION

Regardless of different race histories around the world, this line of invasive questioning is nothing new for mixed folk in many countries. It's been heavily normalised in the past as something we should simply accept and just answer compliantly.

Bear in mind that this was in 1991, but in an infamous viral clip on *Oprah*, Mariah Carey jokes about white people wondering if she is Black and Black people wondering if she is white. Oprah then rolls her eyes comedically and sincerely asks Mariah 'So what arrrre you?'[5] To which the audience laughs along. Mariah ever so obediently, but somewhat wearily, responds with a breakdown of her Venezuelan, Scottish and Black American heritage. I cannot imagine what it must have felt like having to answer *that* question in front of a studio audience on the highest rated talk show at the time, but thankfully Mariah has avidly and defiantly spoken about her mixed identity in her music, her candidly honest autobiography *The Meaning of Mariah Carey* and most recently on Meghan Markle's *Archetypes* podcast. Admittedly I have spent most of my life doing what Mariah did in that moment too, holding the baggage and awkwardness of that question as my duty and responding in full, doing my best to help explain the complications of my race to others to assist them in comprehending the problem of my confusing exterior.

In the past I would laugh along with people's comments about me: *'Don't worry!'* I would say, trying to ease the second-hand embarrassment, *'Nobody else can tell either!'* – offering to carry the burden of my ambiguity on their behalf, as if it was somehow all my fault that I don't make 'racial sense' to anyone. Watching this clip of Mariah I feel a lot of grief for my younger self who went through this incessantly over and over without knowing how to advocate for myself.

In her 2021 book *Mixed/Other*, Natalie Morris exemplifies the weariness and frustration so many of us feel about the burdensome questions.

> *How about instead of society obsessing over whether we are more of one thing or another, we instead develop a better understanding and acceptance of what it means to sit between the two, to belong to both or neither categories?*[6]

PROLONGED RACIAL INTERROGATION IS *STRESSFUL*

Lydia Puricelli (aka the Conscious Culture Coach) is a mixed and multi-ethnic anti-racist trainer and therapist. She is of Indian, Italian and Irish ancestry, born in the UK. Growing up in Southeast London in the 1980s and 90s, she explains the experience many of us share of being racially interrogated since we were very young and its subsequent impact on her.

'It's something that's bothered me my whole life,' says Lydia. 'I would get constantly asked "What are you?" "Where are you from?" And that look that people would give me – a look of confusion like "What is IT?!!"' Lydia describes the assaulting experience of this intrusive interrogation from a young age, dating as far back as primary school before becoming more prevalent in her early teens.

'It's also the way it's asked, when it's asked', Lydia continues, 'because people will say it as the first thing or the second thing they're asking. I felt very different from everyone because nobody was asking anyone else this question, you know, and it wasn't relevant to anyone else.'

Lydia exclaims:

For most people they could just say they are white British, but I have got to explain this whole big story, HUGE paragraphs, and other people can explain using one or two words. I've got to use about four sentences to explain to you 'what I am' so that they can understand. I used to just say I'm Indian, English, Italian and sometimes I'd say Irish depending on my mood. But I had to come up with that myself – my parents didn't teach me to say that, I taught myself.

This raises an important point, that most of us do not have the language to articulate *who we are* at a young age, let alone the complexity of being mixed. Children of colour might all struggle with racial stress, but some will at least have a family to go home to that understands and relates to their experience, whereas Lydia says she tried to navigate such complex racial questions as a child alone by 'sitting with the stress of it', later creating a sort of comedy to avoid the questions.

'Because I'm bright, I just came up with a joke and [would] say "when I grow up I'll have a business card with a pie-chart on it. And I'll get those printed up when I'm older and be able to just give them out"', says Lydia. 'Over time I could get quite angry and I've had arguments with other people of colour, because they were not mixed, or not mixed in the way that I am – so when they have to answer questions, it might have been a little clearer for them to articulate.'

Lydia learned early on how, emotionally, being mixed can feel like a full time job without a map. It reminds me of when people joke about biracial being 'your whole personality'. For some, we have *had* to learn to navigate not only being a person of colour, but also how to decipher biracial life by chronically overthinking because of being interrogated at every turn.

'The whole thing that people need to understand when you're asking that question is how it's so invasive. It is personal. It is painful,' says Lydia. 'What I experienced at home was isolation, racism, prejudice and disconnection (as mixed children will sometimes grow up experiencing this all of this within their own family unit, as we learn more about in the next chapter) – they were reminding me of my lack of sense of identity and my lack of sense of self by asking me these questions. And people have no idea what it means to me to ask these questions. It is none of anyone's business!!'

For Lydia, the questioning brought further complications of having to explain that her cultural identity is different to what is expected if she explains her ethnic identity, creating distress for her.

My stepmother who brought me up is Mauritian-Creole and racially Black, so that is my cultural identity, whilst my biological mother's ethnic identity is Indian-Punjabi, but I'm much more connected to Creole culture. I get it that sometimes for some people, it's all neatly and easily explained but not for me, and that's not who I am. And what happens is that people make assumptions or ideas about me that don't add up to 'what' I actually am.

How to respond to multiracial interrogation

Take a moment

You don't need to answer immediately – *or at all!* Take a deep breath and let the sense of urgency drop away. Now you can consider what's being asked of you and who's asking. Do you know them, or are they a complete stranger? Is this a question you feel comfortable answering? Taking a moment to check in with your emotions can help you let go of the immediate panic and take stock of the situation to find balance before deciding whether to answer. **Dissociation** feels like a kind of involuntary mind and body detachment due to too much stress where you feel numb or zoned out. If you notice this happening, try touching a surface to ground yourself and take a few slow deep breaths. Remember you can take as much time as you need in your decision.

Affirming your position

Allow yourself full permission to decline answering if you feel what is being asked is racist or simply inappropriate, even if the person thinks they are being friendly. Consider how this feels for you – is it comfortable or challenging? If you don't want to answer and that feels difficult to express, you may want to think about your boundaries and how you might learn to feel safe holding firm on them in future.

Boundaries are the emotional limit we place around ourselves to show others what feels OK to us and what doesn't. Mixed people in particular struggle with defining our boundaries because we are so used to being told what our identity is by others. You could explore learning your limits of what feels OK for you personally with a therapist or by practising simply saying 'no' out loud and asserting your limits clearly to others.

Responding on your own terms

Sometimes you may decide the question is innocent and you feel comfortable responding. Less is more, and gives you space to consider these conversations in your own time. Remember you have control over how much information you want to share about your identity! You can always choose to disclose more at a later date when you see them again, or you can decide that you've told them as much as you feel OK sharing and leave it at that. Disclosing your identity – or not – is always your own choice!

REFLECTION

1. Have you ever discussed being racially interrogated with anyone before?
2. How have you responded in the past?
3. Looking back, would you like to change how you respond in the future?

Chapter 2

Family challenges + confusing obstacles

UNSEEN ISSUES OF GROWING UP IN A MULTIRACIAL FAMILY

I keep catching my mother looking for reflections,
glimpses of ghosts in me.
My face is a canvas she can't paint herself into.
'MY MOTHER'S WHITE DAUGHTER', CEILIDH ASHCROFT

My parents fell in love rather innocently, in the 1970s when young lovers were immersed in the idealism prevalent in much of the hippy dippy music and art of the time. Underlying everything, they also both had intergenerationally traumatic war and post-colonisation heritages – Dad's from being an Auschwitz survivor as a baby and Mum's as a young woman during the emergence of the Sri Lankan civil war, rife with intermittent bomb scares.

Even though they never told me this, I sense my parents were unconsciously repressing the breath-stopping weightiness of their own backgrounds and counterbalancing it with the escapist joy of having children. Not much pressure there, then! When I have brought up my multiraciality with my mum, she has shared with me that she envisioned the 1969 hit song 'Melting Pot' by UK band Blue Mink, where metaphorically 'adventurous' lyrics are read in the style of an earnestly rose-tinted human recipe, such as 'take a pinch of white man' and 'wrap it up in Black skin'.[1] Watching a video of the song I can genuinely see how my mum would have been inspired by the pretty Black lady in a sparkly outfit dueting with the hirsute white man, growing up as she did at a time when Asian people – especially darker-skinned curly-haired South Asians like Mum – were racialised as Black (and who also saw themselves as politically Black). Both had tremendous soulful voices and abundantly earnest hopefulness, much like my sweet and musically gifted parents, who fell in love over a shared interest in blues and rock 'n' roll.

As a child of an interracial marriage, I do feel a bit mortified at how naive the song is in romanticising a production line of mixed children with the implication that we will somehow ease racial discord through our existence. The chorus goes: 'What we need is a great big melting pot, Big enough to take the world and all it's got, Keep it stirring for a hundred years or more, And turn out coffee-coloured people by the score.' I definitely do think it's a beautiful thing when people from different cultures get together! But if they are considering having mixed children, they *must* be ready, willing and invested in doing their own inner work around race and racism. As one of those 'coffee-coloured children' I appreciate it was a different time and after the horrors of war, slavery and colonisation, trying to solve everything through a kind of earnestly hapless, racially bypassed type of celebration probably felt like a great idea at the time. Nonetheless, 'Melting Pot' has now been banned from Gold Radio, a British station, for its descriptions of 'curly latin kinkies' and 'yellow chinkies', speaking to the problematic nature of interracial relationships that lack any real conversations. Because the truth is, when children like me were born back then, far from ending racism with our presence, we more often than not got called 'mongrels' or 'half-castes' and ended up without the tools to navigate any of it.

Ignoring the racial differences between a mixed race child and both of their parents doesn't prepare them for racism, or the way the world will forcefully endeavour at every stage of their life journey to interrogate, question and scrutinise their mixed identity (as we saw in the last chapter). Without navigational tools or some helpful direction from our parents, we are adrift at sea and naturally might struggle in some capacity. Those *choosing* to have kids in interracial relationships should consider where parenting might be racially insufficient, for the benefit of their child. Because if mixed and multiracial identity is not adequately reflected during child development years, their sense of self may feel diminished and this will be in danger of becoming intensified when a child will inevitably be met with enquiries and expectations to self-affirm who they are from monoracial society.

In legendary singer, songwriter and producer Mariah Carey's

autobiography, she discusses how herself, her brother and her sister *all* struggled when they weren't accepted by either the white or Black kids. Alongside trauma and poverty, her heartbreaking story speaks to a lack of leadership from either parent in seeing their mixed children's identities clearly and a distinct absence in supporting them in it. Mariah seems *hyper*-aware of the racial differences between herself and her parents and shares how she wouldn't dance in front of her Black dad as a little girl because she feared it as 'a measurement for Black acceptance' whilst her white mother allowed her to go to school with matted hair (fun fact: Mariah also says this is why she loves to use wind machines in videos and photoshoots to celebrate her glorious golden mane!). Mixed children urgently need the tools to *build* the inner psychological ground to take ownership and pride of their mixed identity, and this begins with conscious parenting.

MIXED CHILDREN ARE RACIALLY DIFFERENT TO BOTH PARENTS

In his HBO documentary *1000% Me: Growing Up Mixed*, monoracial Black American comedian and filmmaker W. Kamau Bell interviews children aged 7–16, including three of his own, to try and better understand their world through their eyes. W. Kamau Bell discusses how he and his white partner consciously prepared for their mixed children by fully educating themselves, with his wife studying how to style and care for Black hair properly, something which often gets ignored, causing untold distress to Black mixed children.

W. Kamau Bell told CBS Morning of his first daughter: 'It was about understanding this kid was going to be different than us, and preparing for it so we could envelop her.'[2] W. Kamau Bell's ideas around what to do for his child were developed through truly listening to his daughter's mixed perspective and his talking to his mixed friends. 'I've heard from a lot of mixed race adults who felt like they were cut off from a side of their race because maybe that parent wasn't around, [or] that parent didn't push their culture. So I think a lot of mixed kids want to engage with all sides of what their identity is,' he explains.

1000% Me recognises something really important, that as a mono-racial parent, telling your children they are only one of their races is something they will be reckoning with themselves one day, no matter how they appear to look on the outside. The likelihood is there will be emotional distress and grief, no matter how delayed it is, later in adulthood. Responsible parenting can and must absolutely address how the child appears externally in the eyes of the world, whilst *also* honouring and addressing their internal ethnicity, to teach them that they are *all* of these parts united.

Having mixed children is also an opportunity for not only both parents but both sides of the family to explore important race conversations further, in service to the children and their own anti-racist learning. White parents can take the opportunity to work on their own blindspots and education around racism, whilst the parent of colour might explore their own racial trauma, prejudices and experiences with 'colourism' – discrimination against darker skin shades in a hierarchy of skin tones that often plays out inside BIPOC communities. You can learn more about colourism in Chapter 6.

BEING COMPASSIONATELY CRITICAL

Some might feel bittersweet reading this, as many of us are *still* navigating our recovery from the unintentional neglect of having aspects of our identity unseen by our parents and caregivers. But we must remember that older generations just didn't have the insight or knowledge available today around anti-racism. Post-Black Lives Matter, we do understand a lot more about how systemic and interpersonal race relations, racism, colonisation and slavery have operated in the past, and we have a much greater awareness of how they still lurk in the shadows. Today there are a multitude of books and resources for all parents to learn from, so there are no longer excuses not to do your research!

I'm mindful of how fearful people are to critique their parents. As a therapist and a client of years of therapy, I have realised how important it is in helping provide understanding of our own mixed experience. In a heartfelt and challenging conversation with his parents for the BBC1 documentary 'Stories' series, British South Asian, Kenyan and Jamaican diversity and inclusion facilitator Bilal Harry Khan and his parents discuss topics like: 'Have you ever felt pressured to call out both anti-Blackness in the Asian community, as well as anti-Asian sentiments in the Black community?' and 'Is there anyone on either side of the family who disapproves of my existence?'[3]

Bilal's parents seem pretty clued up, and opening up these kinds of conversations isn't always possible for everyone of course, but considering what you might like to discuss with your parents or caregivers, and what you would like to tell them about how you grew up and how you feel about how you were parented as a mixed child, is something you can reflect on. You can be grateful for the things your parents taught you and provided you with, whilst also allowing yourself to feel anger, frustration and grief about what their parenting lacked.

Many parents may not have understood their own racial experiences, let alone the impact of their cultural crossover in an interracial partnership. Like many baby boomers, my parents had an aversion to emotional closeness and open communication styles, demonstrating their love instead through material legacy and stoicism. To use a cliché, my parents 'did their best with the tools they had available', and sitting with the discomfort of this is something I constantly endeavour to come to terms with. I have achieved this through trying to understand what they *also* went through. Consider what our parents were maybe struggling with themselves – racism, undiagnosed trauma, stress, disabilities, undiagnosed neurodivergence, immigration, no internet! etc. – all of these would impact how consciously caregivers are able to parent. We must keep on remembering these interrelated issues that may all add up to mixed children not being adequately supported, whilst also pushing for society and parents to do better.

Becoming more conscious and unpacking my own experiences in therapy has been a privilege in many ways, one that parents who are too busy operating in survival mode often do not have available to them. By considering all of this you can learn to hold immense compassion for your parents/caregivers whilst also acknowledging that you have every right to feel frustration, sadness and pain at what was neglected around your mixed identity when they were raising you.

Some of my challenges with growing up mixed were as follows: both my parents called me 'white'. Compared to my dark-brown-skinned mother I was very light, and I can see why my parents may have done that based on how I appeared to them. But when I went to school the children could see I was not white and I was racially abused. This was extremely confusing as I didn't even know what my race was, because my parents hadn't told me I was mixed. Yet suddenly I had to deal with various racial slurs, and of course I felt all the pain of it, regardless of not understanding any of it.

This lack of clarity around my own racial identity was exacerbated when I got a bit older. Mum volunteered in my middle school library, which became somewhere I used to avoid when I knew she was there to prevent more interrogation from classmates by drawing attention to myself and my mum. Mum must have sensed something was up by how cagey and quiet I very often was when she was in school, but she avoided calling me out on it. Looking back, I wish we could have had an open conversation together to release the racial shame that I was carrying for the both of us. I'm sure Mum's naive hope was that I would never experience racism at all because of the way I looked compared to her, but I just experienced a different incarnation of racism instead.

Writing a therapeutic letter to your parents

We don't always get the opportunity to tell our parents or care-givers everything we would like to say about how we feel about how they parented us as a mixed child. But it can really help to write them a letter of what you would like to say.

- This doesn't need to be something that you send, but rather something you can use to release difficult feelings or even just to understand your feelings around how you were parented as a mixed child.
- Try to tell the truth of what you feel about your experiences when you write it, which might be hard!
- Once you have written the letter, keep it somewhere safe so you can read it a few times to absorb and reflect on what happened – it might be useful to read it out to your therapist (if you have one) and discuss it.
- You can carry on writing new versions of the therapeutic letter if you have more to express and add over time.

MIXED + MULTIRACIAL IDENTITY DEVELOPMENT

Dr Jenn Noble is an African American and Tamil-Sri Lankan psy-chologist, parent coach, college professor and founder of the Free to Be Collective and The Mixed Life Academy. She is based in South

California. While writing this book, I wanted to chat with her about the little-understood area of mixed identity development – a concept first introduced by W.S. Carlos Poston in 1990 demonstrating how multiracial challenges can successfully be supported to develop a healthy and robust mixed identity. As a pioneer of this field, Dr Jenn has specialised in helping parents find the tools to raise confident mixed kids.

Dr Jenn: The search that's going to happen at the age of identity development [is] more complicated, a bit more taxing [for mixed and multiracial kids] because finding your identity as an adolescent, whether you're monoracial or not, is already hard work. You've got to figure out 'OK, who am I?' 'Do I want to be like my parents?' But when you don't have the information to go off, you have to scramble around to find it.

Namalee: Scramble is the word! My personal and clinical experience is that many mixed people lack identity support from their parents – what are your thoughts as a parent coach?

Dr Jenn: Certainly for some mixed race kids, that didn't get any help with this – when the time comes for them to navigate and figure out who they are, they might feel like, 'I never got to learn about this culture,' 'I don't know how to connect to this part... but everybody thinks I'm "this" so I'll just go with [it].' They might assume 'They don't know what I am, they just think I'm white. So I'll just live that way.' 'I'll just try to be raceless and blend in as much as possible, because I don't know how to do this really humongous task of connecting to this culture.'

So they may just skip [developing their identity], or try to skip it. But multiracial identity is really not skippable, so that's why I say – it becomes increasingly more complicated because you can pretend that you can skip it. [But] if you do that it's gonna appear in a different way [as an issue].

Namalee: Yes, there really is this danger of erasing an entire part of who a child is, in order to make themselves racially fit in a way that is not in service to themselves, if the parents aren't 'multiracial aware'. I think that's what I tried to do as a child – because my parents didn't discuss anything at all with me and so I didn't feel I had permission to speak to them about anything that involved my mixed race reality. They just projected their ideas onto me and I got the message I had to be fine all the time, because they were stressed and I didn't want to make things worse for them, and of course it's my parents, I just believed everything they taught me, as you do...!

Dr Jenn: Being mixed just complicates so much of the identity process. Whereas having those important conversations allows that child to get to adolescence and then go, 'Oh, okaaaaay. My parents have been telling me I'm this AND this, AND that. So now let me incorporate how I want to move forward with this knowledge.' It's very important!

Namalee: Yes, it's creating an 'inner ground' for your child so they can internalise some positive racial and cultural stability within themselves, rather than always having to search outside themselves for approval for who they are as mixed kids. If there's an inner ground to stabilise them, it leaves room for them to make the decision to choose which direction to go in, rather than flailing all over the place not really knowing how or trying to do it, because maybe, like me, you were trying to hide racism that you pretended hadn't happened!

Dr Jenn: Right! So many go through that. You must have just internalised a whole bunch of other people's messages, all without an adult challenging that. Because that's what kids do, they're gonna hear a bunch of stuff and internalise it until someone's like, 'you know, that's not right'. It just gets internalised, until a parent or a parental figure/caregiver behaves in that parental way and stops it. If you're not told that as a child, it builds up, and builds up! And the child gets completely overwhelmed with this strange racial messaging.

HELPING YOUR MIXED + MULTIRACIAL CHILD TO SEE THEMSELVES

It's important that a parent helpfully reflects to the child that they are OK and acceptable exactly as they are, for the child to get a sense of *who* they are and to help build their self-esteem. **Mirroring** is a therapy term that isn't about physical mirroring in the way we might think of a reflection in a mirror, but rather it's about how our interactions and communication reflect on a child as an act of affirming them. Think about how *you* feel when you are given praise and how it makes you more confident in yourself and who you are. If racial identity is not *mirrored* by the adult, then a child may not be able to 'see' themselves, and they might be confused at the mixed racial messaging.

If, like many of us, you literally did not know *what* you were so that you could explain it to others, it might lead to internalising this racial ambiguity as something that is *your own fault*. As I mentioned earlier, my parents not explaining my multiraciality to me led to me feeling shame when I received questions that I didn't know how to answer. So few of us get taught how to navigate this, but when mixed children do have their experience adequately mirrored to them by parents or caregivers who demonstrate racial awareness and understanding for the entirety of their mixed identity, this can provide and build the internal compass we really need.

Meryl Fernandes is a TV presenter and pub owner, of British Goan-Indian, monoracial heritage. Here she describes how she mirrors her seven-year old mixed daughter's experience, whilst also being authentic and positive about how she experiences her daughter's difference to her.

'Her school is very multiracial!!' says Meryl. 'The majority are non-white. And most are mixed. I've taught her to say she's "both". We use that language now – it's like, when we talk about gender she would say "he, she and they", yeah, that's her language. That is her "normal".'

When her daughter goes to school, she sees other children who are mixed like her and her multicultural identity is celebrated and openly discussed so there is further mirroring from this socialised experience of school too. Meryl acknowledges her daughter is having a different experience of celebrating her South Asian heritage that wasn't available to Meryl growing up. 'There were zero discussions about culture, Asian or African history at my primary school, so it was hard to feel pride, as it was never celebrated.'

Finding healing in helping her mixed daughter feel proud of who she is culturally is something Meryl couldn't access at that age due to racism she experienced herself. Her daughter, who is light-skinned, is experiencing racial safety in the care of her mother, despite presenting as *racially different* to her because her mother is 'mirroring' being mixed and celebrating this aspect to her child. The awareness given to her daughter's mixed culture affirms to her that being of both of her heritages is normalised, and something to be proud of. This considerate language creates emotional security for her child, although it hasn't been easy for Meryl, who works to consciously separate out her own experiences of trauma from her child's experiences.

I feel like I get these triggers off her based on emotional flashbacks to my own childhood. We'll cook a curry, and we live in a small flat, and I'll grab her uniform, and I'll put it in the cupboard so that none of her school clothes will smell. Because I remember that dreadful feeling of going to school and smelling of onions. And I remember the first time I did this, and my husband was like, 'What are you doing?!!' And I was like, 'I don't want her to smell of curry!'

The open communication around race between Meryl and her white partner Tom meant that he immediately noticed the racism fear in his wife for her child because of trauma she had been through herself, and he could provide support. 'Tom said to me, "Our daughter is PROUD of her curry!!" It's so nice, because that chills me out about my childhood.'

Having a child that looks completely different to her brought up some challenging feelings for Meryl about racism that she endured herself. She speaks courageously of visceral feelings about how her child looked in comparison to her immediately after giving birth. 'It was so weird to see a pink baby come out of me. And also she was the spitting image of my husband's white dad. So, I've just given birth to a mini father-in-law!!' Meryl laughs. She continues:

Women talk about this euphoria, but I didn't have that at all. There was a lot going on – this pink and white body emerging from my dark skinned body! ... Obviously, I was completely in love with her, but I was in shock at what she looked like and how pink she was. This real moment of laying her on my chest and her just being a completely different colour. I just thought she'd be darker, and I thought she'd be more of a mix of us, so I was like 'wow there's this pink thing on my dark, black nipple' – it just threw me a bit. I felt I couldn't talk about it to anyone. But of course – it's a huge privilege to be a mother and have a healthy baby!

When racism and colourism exist in society, giving birth to a baby that looks so racially different might naturally bring up traumatic memories or feelings about a parent's own experiences.

Meryl recalls that later when she took her newborn out for walks, 'Lots of people thought I was the nanny and I remember being really thrown by it initially.'

Childbirth and parenthood is a huge adjustment, and parents like Meryl routinely encounter extra challenges through these kinds of outsider reactions, which can make a BIPOC parent even more aware of their own identity, the racism of others and the phenotype differences between parent and child.

The BAFTA nominated playwright and director Gabriel Bisset-Smith, who is of white English, Scottish and Jamaican heritage, wrote *Whitewash*, a semi-autobiographical play that explored his relationship with his Black mixed mother and what it was like for her to have a white-presenting baby. In a video about *Whitewash* for the Soho Theatre, Gabriel's mother Jenny describes how she was also asked if she was the nanny. 'I was always either "the carer" or "the nanny". People used to argue with me about whose child he was.'[4] When strangers impose this kind of racism on mixed families, it is distressing for both the parent and developing child alike.

Roxanne Murray is a white Irish and Black Bajan queer disability activist and one of BBC's '2024 100 women of the year'. Born and raised in West London, Roxanne points out an extremely confusing and painful incident for her and her white mum:

By the time I was 10 or 11, I started to feel the weight of these [race] dynamics more acutely. Puberty brought a greater awareness of the world around me. People were less shy about voicing their real thoughts. One experience that stuck with me was an encounter with members of the Nation of Islam in a lift at a nearby estate. They called my mum the 'White devil' while simultaneously trying to embrace me, as though rejecting half of who I was wouldn't affect me!

Projecting onto us that we don't belong with our own parents feels like nothing new for mixed people who grow up with the perma-stares and tone-deaf comments from the general public. In 2023, *The Independent* newspaper reported, 'parents of biracial children are increasingly being accused of human trafficking on flights by fellow passengers and airline staff'. Mixed children are being traumatised because outsiders can't fathom our interracial families. When outsiders interfere in the bond between mother/father and child, it could create difficult feelings between them that might be repressed in the relationship. This is exactly why racial and cultural attunement between parent and child (where the child feels racially and culturally safe in their parents' presence and care) is immensely important!

Sophie Kanno, who you met last chapter, is conscious that being mixed has been challenging for her growing up as a child who is racially different to both her parents:

I needed to find community but I knew I was not going to find someone who is exactly like me with my parents' exact story. I live on the West Coast now where there's a great Japanese-American community, but I didn't grow up in that – I grew up on the East Coast and most people were Chinese, Vietnamese or Filipino. There were Asians, but there weren't Asians who were 'like me'. I actually ended up gravitating more towards the Black and brown people just because I felt there was more understanding there. I think it had to do with the fact that my mother is white, and there was more safety in being around their [Black and brown] mothers and their family because they weren't going to perpetuate white supremacy and microaggressions.

Although they don't understand the complexities of race, children easily pick up on the *feeling* of danger or lack of safety from racism by how their parents respond and try to protect them. Sophie further explains how she felt understandably distraught about trying to navigate her multiracial identity growing up amidst the confusing messages around race that she later unpacked in adulthood:

I, like most kids like me, felt a sense of betrayal that my parents didn't prepare me or my three siblings at all for this experience. It was really hard and I had to do a lot of work on learning why I was so upset with them. I just felt so let down and betrayed and it really was like setting us up for failure. Unfortunately, when I reflect back on it, my mom centred herself by saying things like 'people never think you're my kids and I never think I'm your mom', etc., and it's like I know that that's hard for her too but there is a space for that and it should not dominate the conversation in the household.

As the BIPOC parent, Sophie's father was preoccupied with his own model minority struggles, which many monoracial immigrants of colour have to deal with. 'My father, being an Asian immigrant, was like, "I've just gotta focus on work and practising my English. I can't complain about this either, I can't even acknowledge it." It's the immigrant mentality, you know.'

THE IMPORTANCE OF RACIAL SAFETY IN ATTACHMENT STYLE

We cannot underestimate the impact of racial attachment to our own parents in the mixed identity development process, especially when, like Sophie explains, both parents are racially different to their mixed child. As a therapist who works with trauma I am often checking in with all my clients to see if they feel 'safe' – but what does that mean exactly? Emotional or psychological safety is a peaceful, calm state within all humans when our sympathetic and parasympathetic nervous systems are working in balance, helping us to easily return to an emotionally regulated inner state. When we feel accepted, respected, seen, understood and authentically listened to we all feel an internal felt sense of calm throughout our body and psyche. In this state we can freely express our thoughts, feelings and needs without fear of danger, judgement or punishment.

Hyper-vigilance is when we feel on guard and anxious. Mixed children who are hyper-vigilant are often waiting to see which racial side they are expected to perform for parents and family. **Code-switching** is something all marginalised identities do and describes swapping one identity for another to stay emotionally safe, to blend in and to please the status quo. Code-switching might happen as a result of hyper-vigilance when mixed children learn to perform one racial mask for one side of the family and another for the other side, rarely finding the safe opportunity to become their whole, racially integrated self.

Multiracial Attachment Styles

Attachment styles are rooted in evidence-based research where children need to secure a close bond with parents and caregivers for survival purposes before they can then move on to healthy identity development stages. I have created an adaptation tailored especially for mixed and multiracial people to show how attachment styles might interact with the mixed aspect of your identity. You may be a combination of styles at different times.

Secure

- You feel comfortable and safe in human interactions with an abundance of trust in relationships that comes naturally because bonds with your parent(s) and caregiver(s) were consistent and racially safe.
- You are able to talk about being mixed/BIPOC and how you feel about it without fear of reprisal from parents and/or community.
- Feeling like your true self comes naturally because you mostly felt racially safe, seen and validated growing up.

Anxious

- You may be unsure about how much of your mixed self you can actually be in relationships so you cling to others with people-pleasing behaviour or trying to bargain, so that you can stay safe and be accepted by your community.
- Maybe your parents get things right with race on occasion, but sometimes they don't, so you frequently question if you are doing or saying the correct thing in different racial contexts for fear of offending or being ostracised.
- You may 'code-switch' for different family members and take on a people-pleasing, performative way of being.
- You may find it challenging to be your authentic mixed self.

Avoidant

- You know that parents/family/caregivers were racially unsafe for you to be around so you create distance between yourself and them to avoid being further hurt or rejected.
- Maybe your parents 'don't see colour', are 'tone deaf' and/or do not recognise your specific needs as a mixed child. This causes you to feel unprotected and/or vulnerable

and so you learn to protect yourself through distancing and isolating yourself from parents and/or community.

Disorganised

- You have suffered some form of racist abuse and/or microaggressions from parents, caregivers or family which has confused you regarding who is safe to be around and who isn't. You may also experience this in your community, who you might feel afraid of as you feel you will probably be rejected.
- You never feel 'racially safe' at home and therefore do not know how to attain racial safety in wider social contexts as you lack self-esteem and self-trust in your mixed identity.

WHY WE NEED *THE TALK* FOR MIXED CHILDREN TOO

The Talk is a conversation given to Black and brown children by racially responsible parents to prepare them for how the world will treat them differently as the result of racism. If you are a Black or brown child whose parents have given you *The Talk*, it will give you a good start with a large aspect of who you are and how to protect yourself, particularly for Black children. Farzana Nayani is a diversity and inclusion specialist of Filipina and Pakistani heritage, whose book *Raising Mixed and Multiracial Children: Tools for Nurturing Identity in a Racialized World* (2020) asserts that a separate version of *The Talk* is also desperately needed for all mixed and multiracial children to explain how the world will respond to them for being mixed.

Alex Lewis is a British-born psychotherapist of Jamaican and English/Scottish heritage who grew up in Peterborough, England. Here he describes some of the complications associated with this identity when Alex's Jamaican dad gave him his version of *The Talk*:

When I was younger he always said, 'You are Black, you've got to work twice as hard as everyone else'. He said all the things you would expect an old

Jamaican man to say to his son. So when I got to about 14 or 15 I really leaned into my Blackness and I started to do a lot more research and I visited my granddad and I just started to identify with my Blackness and my Jamaican side as well, because that's where my roots are. I've only been to Jamaica once, but it's still a part of me.

Alex approached his dad with his developing thoughts:

I remember when I was 16 or 17 I went up to my dad and said, 'Yeah, I'm Black!!!' And I remember him saying, 'No, you're not!' after a whole lot of my dad telling me I'm Black. And I was SO confused. He said, 'No, no, you're mixed race – you're English!' and I'm like but you've literally told me my whole life 'I'm Black'??

By the time Alex took ownership of his Blackness, in his own way, his dad had changed his mind:

Before that it was always just him almost lecturing me about Blackness and saying you've got to be careful. But then, when I started to lean into my Blackness and just call myself Black and really own it and be like, 'I'm a young black boy,' then he was 'No, you're not.' It still triggers me today as something that I need to be wary of.

Alex's own life experience is of being Black-presenting and racialised outside the family, as a Black man. 'I'm Black British – I really feel like this term resonates with me. This is what I really am.'

Alex's mixed identity seems to have confused his father, who was not equipped to understand it, and in his confusion he unknowingly transferred that to Alex as his *own* problem to deal with. Alex's story demonstrates how mixed children's identity might trigger monoracial parents' own unconscious identity issues, and reiterates how there is a need for a separate version of *The Talk* about being mixed, as Alex had to navigate that part of his identity alone.

No time like the present
Don't wait until 'something happens' to have this conversation with them – the earlier the better. It will just feel more natural

for them and for you! Explain to them they are both (or all) of their heritages and reinforce how wonderful this is. You could warmly point out differences between them and you whilst also reinforcing similarities between you both, letting them know that our differences make us special. There are many mixed identity children's books (see Chapter 12) that you can start reading with them from an early age, which can help make things more playful and fun.

Affirm their mixed identity

Affirm their mixed identity to them when they seem confused so that they know all the elements they are mixed with and let them know they can choose how they wish to identify. Tell them that their Black or non-Black identity also might be responded to differently by different folk, and that other people's opinion is never a reflection on their self-worth or value.

Teach them positive boundaries

Let them know that the outside world may try to challenge, question and police their mixed identity so gently guide them on what they might say and how to have firm boundaries when people try to interrogate them. This could be achieved in a playful way if they are young or maybe with role play of how to self-affirm and speak up when they are a bit older (see Chapter 1).

Provide a safe space

Let them know it's OK to bring home and share difficult feelings about what peers, bullies or strangers say to them about being mixed – and demonstrate that home is always a safe space to explore this together.

Give them plenty of choice with firm guidance

Reinforce that the child's racial identity is fluid and ever changing if they wish; that the way they want to describe themselves is always up to them and it's not for anybody else to dictate to them. Reinforce that they might decide to change how they identify over time.

WHEN RACISM IS NORMALISED INSIDE THE HOME

Focusing on all the shiny, appealing aspects of the mixed experience is commonly favoured by those not mixed themselves. Saying things like we have 'the best of both worlds', which could be true in some circumstances, ignores the reality that many of us also experience the worst of both worlds as well.

Pauline Jérémie is the creator of *Middleground,* an art and literature magazine for mixed people (more on this in Chapter 9). She is of French and Caribbean heritage and suffered repetitive explicit racial abuse from her white French mother and extended white family in France which, in common with the British Empire, has a cultural undercurrent of colonisation:

I'm French and my dad was from Martinique in the West Indies (a French colony). My father was Black Caribbean and my mother is white, originally from Brittany. My parents divorced when I was six and my father passed when I was 11 and we lost contact with his side of the family. My entire upbringing was with my white mother, her white family, my white stepfather and his white family. There was no representation of Blackness when I was growing up at all. Not that it wasn't spoken about, and not that people assumed I was white within my family. We were very aware that my sister and I were mixed but it was like, [we were] only theoretically [mixed] when it comes to the way we were treated.

Pauline doesn't recall how early the racism started:

Mum called me the N-word. And she couldn't understand when I said I didn't want to be called that. We had many arguments where she stated that she should be allowed to say whatever she wanted, because it's 'just a word' – and she said it is what I am. She said that making it taboo was causing more racism than not using the word!

Pauline's stoic approach towards her mother's racism demonstrates the compartmentalising and bargaining with a parent that may happen to ease the developmental racial trauma, and what becomes normalised in a mixed child, before they even step foot outside of the house. Trying to negotiate parental racism becomes a necessary skill. Because what else are you going to do when the people meant to protect you are racist to you as a growing child?

My mother has a complete lack of understanding about racial history and the weight of that word, which even, as a person of Black heritage, I do not use. I completely understand Black people wanting to reclaim it, as I think it's mine to reclaim. So there was just the complete rejection of my emotions and experiences. And it started happening more after George Floyd passed. We had our last big argument just before the pandemic, and we didn't speak for months. It was so weird for me to navigate, even though I have the privilege of being light-skinned – I was having to deal with this.

Pauline describes how she felt, coping by trying to teach her mother and taking on the role of anti-racism educator in the face of a racist power dynamic in her own home.

It was really isolating, I had no mixed friends and my sister and I have a strained relationship and she's disabled and doesn't fully understand racism. We were very much alone. I felt unsafe with my family; I felt that I couldn't bring up race. I managed to convince my mum to read Why I'm No Longer Talking to White People About Race when it came out in French and the only thing she told me afterwards was, 'Wow, it really reminds me of what your dad and I went through.' And I thought, 'You didn't go through any of that. HE did!' I just kind of stay away from that topic now because I don't feel safe bringing it up.

Racism within the home is far more common than many realise, and it is not something limited to any specific part of the world, as US rapper Logic discusses in his song 'Mixed Feelings' where he tells how his white American mother was racist to him when he was growing up too. Logic is often criticised for speaking up so explicitly about being mixed. He has controversially used the N-word in his music, to convey his experience of being called this by his white mother, but it is usually frowned upon by the Black community when someone who is phenotypically white-presenting uses this word. It is not my place as a non-Black, non-American mixed person to have the authority to speak on this, but what I do know is the burden of dealing with interfamilial racism is not for the faint-hearted, and that it is often left up to the victims to work it out alone, in a society that doesn't acknowledge or support the unique racial prejudice mixed people face, in the way it does for other forms of racism. It's perhaps not a surprise that Logic turned to music as a creative outlet to help him make sense of his own harrowing experience.

Alex, who featured earlier in this chapter recounting his dad's confusing version of *The Talk*, also experienced racism from his [mother's] white ex-partner:

> *It was really confusing because there were times when he was quite nice and fatherly and took me on fishing trips. I remember one time my mom was out and he just said to me, 'You're just a little Black bastard.' I didn't tell my mum or my dad. I only told my mum about three or four years ago because I was only like eight or nine at the time. I just remember thinking no one's gonna believe me. So I had to hold that myself as well and as a child. It's not right that you have to live in the house of someone who called you that. I still really want to punch that guy. Because as a child... it's terrible.*

Then there are the microaggressions that are less obvious but still very confusing to experience as a child. Although we don't necessarily understand it at a younger age, we can certainly sense injustice and inequality amongst our parents, and it affects us. When I was little, my dad often spoke about how 'Ceylon' was a Dutch colony and made jokes that my mum was born in a mud hut and wore a grass skirt. I used to laugh along with dad, because my mum laughed too. But as I got older I started to feel annoyed at dad for saying this and also annoyed at my mum for laughing along, even though I couldn't articulate why I felt any of this angst. It just came out in a kind of annoyance at both of them that made me look like a stroppy teenager, when it was actually *way* deeper. How do mixed children learn to develop protection for themselves against microaggressions, if they are taught that within their own family it is acceptable?

BI-CULTURAL, BI-ETHNIC + 'THIRD CULTURE' IDENTITY

You may have heard the expression *third culture kid* which describes someone who grows up with multiple overlapping cultural influences due to being raised in a culture that is different to their parents' original one(s). Being mixed goes hand in hand with having parents from different cultural and/or ethnic backgrounds adding more elements into the mix that provide a unique diversity of influences. For instance, I have a multitude of elements that will have impacted me:

1. Mum is culturally Sri Lankan, Catholic and Buddhist.
2. Dad was culturally Dutch and Jewish.
3. Dad was ethnically Dutch, German and Jewish.
4. Mum is ethnically Sinhalese Sri Lankan.
5. Both were first generation immigrants to the UK.
6. I am British.

My cultural identity is impacted by a unique combination of all these elements mixed together. Those of us who hold multiple cultural identities may have challenging and ever changing relationships with all of our identities, depending on how they have manifested in our lives.

SIBLING STRUGGLES

When siblings are different skin shades, it inevitably results in different racial experiences and different ways of identifying and receiving treatment from family members and society, according to how they look. In true-to-life scenes from British BBC soap drama *Eastenders* in 2024 this was movingly portrayed when mixed Black and white sisters Gina and Anna Knight are forced to reckon with their phenotype (observable) differences leading to unjust treatment in the family from their racist granddad. Gina educates her sister by telling her, 'You pass Anna, you could be white,' to which Anna responds, 'I'm just as Black as you,' to which Gina explains that isn't how the world sees them. Gina, whose hair is closer to a more 'typically' Black hair texture, is picked on, whilst Anna, who is blonde-haired with looser curls, is treated more favourably simply because she looks 'whiter'.[5]

TRANSRACIAL ADOPTEE EXPERIENCE

Transracially adopted children experience some crossovers with multiracial children, due to having caregivers of a different race. Dr Yvon Guest, who is of Jamaican and Irish/English heritage, is a mixed-race therapy expert and creator of Kaleidoscope, an online conference for mixed and multiracial heritage in therapy. Dr Guest has been developing research on mixed identity for over 20 years. She was fostered herself and wrote in *Therapy Today*: 'The white foster parents I lived with for 13 years saved me from an early childhood in institutions. But they also thought they were doing the right thing by ignoring my Caribbean heritage.'[6]

Dr Guest goes on to acknowledge that mixed and Black children in the predominantly white care system can go through a process of 'identity stripping', which she describes as 'racial and cultural isolation' that results in an inability to develop the survival skills needed to navigate a racist society. When mixed and multiracial children are adopted there is also a *double* complexity that must be considered in how they will attach to caregivers and navigate connections with others.

INTERGENERATIONAL TRAUMA

Parents might unknowingly bring children up with the baggage of their own historical lineages unconsciously influencing them in the background. This is known as 'intergenerational/transgenerational trauma', which can occur through ancestral lines. **Epigenetics** is the study of changes where our gene expression has been altered due to trauma that is either inherited biologically and/or passed down via learned behaviours. We may therefore experience traumatic symptoms and patterns that are similar to what our grandparents and ancestors went through, without actually going through the original trauma, because of 'epigenetic inheritance'. This might occur in the form of dissociation, anxiety, night terrors or nightmares, etc. It's something to be mindful of, especially when bringing up mixed children, as the combined intergenerational trauma 'legacies' of our parents might also be in conflict with each other.

In the story of Nigerian and German born Jennifer Teege's book, *My Grandfather Would Have Shot Me: A Black Woman Discovers Her Family's*

Nazi Past, the author grapples with a conflicted intergenerational trauma heritage whilst also being mixed. Intergenerational trauma heritages might include: American slavery, colonialism, World War 2, Windrush, Partition, the Jewish Holocaust, the Irish Potato Famine, the Tamil Genocide, the Palestinian Genocide, the Armenian Genocide, refugee and migration lineages from any war, or traumatic world events such as natural disaster, etc.

MULTIGENERATIONALLY MIXED

This is when families are mixed through the generations – for example through two multiracial people marrying and having multiply-mixed children. This can happen in any country, to the point where no one might know the origins or specific mixes any more. Multigenerational mixed heritage is more prevalent in some countries than in others, where generations of mixing may go far back, for example in South America, where mixing might point to differences in colonisation styles; the Spanish embraced racial mixing in their colonial system, in contrast to the English, Dutch, French, Belgians, etc. who didn't.

Multigenerationally mixed heritage is a broad umbrella term that will look very different depending on where in the world multigenerational mixing occurs. Multigenerationally mixed cultural experience and self-understanding will also differ vastly between countries, depending on specific histories i.e. South Africa, specifically use the term 'colored' rather than 'mixed' for people multigenerationally mixed through the specific political trauma of apartheid, whereas in South America, someone who is multigenerationally mixed would likely be mixed through Spanish colonisation, which was more subtle in it's racial hierarchy 'style', and focused on creating a 'unified' Spanish empire across it's territories.

Jeanneth Lopera is a reiki healer of Colombian heritage who was born in the UK and describes herself as British-Colombian; she says of the internalised racism and colourism she witnesses in her community:

My heritage is colonised, with indigenous, but I describe myself as just Colombian. We know we are 'mestizo' [colonial term for mixed with white] but we do not think of Spain as part of our roots. In Colombia they don't really care, or focus on the mix. It's not relevant to them. But to me it is,

*because there are racists who are against Black and indigenous people –
but they don't make the link of themselves being indigenous mixed with
European heritage.*

Although there is a chance multigenerationally mixed parents are
conscious about the multiracial experience, this isn't always the case,
especially if there is intergenerationally internalised racism through
the lineage as Jeanneth suggests. That is to say, it shouldn't be taken for
granted that just because you have a multigenerationally mixed family
they will *naturally* know how to positively support mixed children.

COMMUNITY AND CONTEXT MATTERS

If a child lacks community at home and then goes to a school in an
area without much multiculturalism or support for their mixed identity, this could affect them too. My parents specifically chose to move
to the countryside with the very best of intentions, for the clean air
and beautiful surroundings. But being present in idyllic surroundings
without many families of colour for support was isolating for a mixed
child like me, who would have benefitted from being around more
multicultural families.

Musician Mabel (Sierra Leonean, Swedish, English and Scottish)
spent her teen years in Sweden before coming to the UK. Mabel told
The Face magazine, 'they don't really have a word for mixed race [in
Sweden]'. Mabel, who has spoken extensively of her anxiety issues,
says: 'I've had a lot of self-worth and confidence issues growing up. I
had a difficult time socially in school. I stopped going at 15 because I
couldn't deal with the idea of what other people may or may not be
thinking.'[7] We cannot underestimate the impact of being *othered*, and
how distressing it can be not to have the language to describe your
mixed experience, when you just simply want to fit in as a teen developing your identity like any other.

Although the various issues might seem challenging to read about
at first, if we embrace some of the tools we discussed in this chapter,
it is absolutely possible to disrupt the cycle of distress for mixed
children and teenagers. Some things, like systemic racism, are beyond
the control of parents, but creating the right foundations for discussions around racism and mixed identity to guide children on how to

navigate the challenges together will go a long way to supporting your mixed child! Mixed and multiracial children, like any other children, don't need *perfect* parents – they just need to feel support, guidance and connection, so that they can feel safely tethered to their family whilst also feeling free to explore the art of becoming themselves out in the world.

REFLECTION

1. Did your parent(s) or caregiver(s) speak to you about being mixed? How was this experience of growing up for you?
2. Have you ever experienced racism or microaggressions from parents or caregivers?
3. Do you think you felt racial safety growing up? Have you ever spoken to anyone about this?
4. Note down the different overlapping ethnicities and cultures that impacted your mixed identity. How did this affect you growing up?
5. What might your parents have done differently to support your mixed identity journey?

Chapter 3

Coming home to your mixed body

EMBRACING HOW YOU FEEL ON THE INSIDE + LOOK ON THE OUTSIDE

My body is not my body –
not just my body –
parts of bodies, other bodies.

I am not quite –
I am not entirely –
You know you kind of look like –
but you know not really –

My body is not my body –
but it is my body –
just a body.

'BODYNOTABODY', HERA HONG

'I find it hard to write about my race, because my feelings are written on my face, white nose, brown eyes, mixed feelings. Choose a side. I can't', says Canadian Gujarati-Indian and English, Irish actor Avan Jogia in his poetry book, *Mixed Feelings*.[1]

Trying to locate a map to our identities through reflecting on our bodies is something we might naturally be preoccupied with. On my first visit to Sri Lanka to meet my extended family, during one trip in the mountains of Kandy, I saw a mural of some flute-playing indigenous women wearing brightly coloured sarongs and dripping in the most epic gold facial jewellery. Studying their pronounced shoulders and curvy structure prompted me to think maybe I do look more Sri Lankan than people realise from just my skin colour. I may be lighter skinned and taller than many Sri Lankans, and yet at 5ft 7ins, Dutch people (who are officially the tallest nation in the world!) have told me I am 'short'. So in which land does my mixed body belong exactly?

When you really want to belong somewhere, anywhere, it can feel alienating to keep being told over and over that you simply don't look like where you originate from. As TikToker Zuri Mullings explains in her video: 'POV: You're mixed race and neither side of your family looks like you', 'Where does that leave you feeling about yourself?'[2] Well... quite!! In the past it has often left me feeling kind of in limbo, sometimes craving fitting in, and at other times completely rebelling. Ambiguous-looking mixed people do have the 'strange bonus' of being able to go to foreign lands and people treating us as one of their own. Like when I travelled to Morocco, Mexico and Brazil and it felt great for a while. Until you realise you can't speak the language and your face and body have rendered you a slow burn imposter there, too!

In the last chapter we discussed how mirroring the mixed child who is seeking to see themselves in their parents soothes them and helps them see themselves clearly. So what can we do to reassure ourselves about our own identity if we don't already have that kind of foundation? I have found creativity to be an extremely helpful tool in the mixed healing process. For me, sometimes poetry or free association writing techniques are truly the only way to express how peculiarly perplexing it is to have such heightened awareness of the mosaic of races visible in different parts of my face and body; and all at once how disembodied and fascinating it can feel.

I wrote a song back in 2008 about feeling like my own features were at war with each other, with lyrics that went 'You and me it's World War 3, eye to eye collide in one body', describing some of the strange, combustive energy I felt back then. Today I recognise these kinds of feelings are completely normal when multiracial people are constantly made to feel we must be one or the other. Dr Yvon Guest, the UK therapist mentioned earlier, developed the concept of a 'no man's land' where mixed people might find themselves having no place of their own, feeling stuck between oppositional worlds.

SEEING YOURSELF CLEARLY – REPRESENTATION

What are mixed children supposed to do when our mixed identity is not being reflected anywhere at all? In *Stylist Magazine* Laila Woozer, a queer, non-binary author and artist of Welsh, French, Scottish, American, Indian and Mauritian heritage, writes of their gratitude for growing up seeing the legendary Spice Girl Mel B. 'The only actual mixed person I knew of was Mel B aka Scary Spice. She had a huge impact on me when I heard her describe herself as having a "brown dad and white mum" on TV – wow, so just like me!'[3]

Laila goes on to say it was still unclear whether there was anyone else. 'As I grew older, I had dozens of unanswered questions: were there other mixed people, or just me and Mel B? Because I couldn't find any representation of myself, I didn't know where I belonged, or what I was supposed to look like.'

Lacking representation and constantly being questioned about my observable phenotype differences as a teenager led to me becoming as intrigued with looking at myself as others were with me! In a way I was reclaiming people's fixation on my appearance as my own. Away from everyone else's opinions, I taught myself to see how much I looked like both my mum *and* my dad, regardless of what anyone said about us, through painting self-portraits over and over. I don't think I did this consciously but looking back I can see how studying my features in detail as I fashioned myself in oil pastels in pinks, beiges, browns and yellows helped me start to recognise that if people couldn't see my mum and dad in me, it was only because they couldn't see beyond our different skin tones.

Painting myself in detail meant I used to constantly look in the mirror as a teenager, and because of this I soon started expanding my interest beyond my face and body, to adorning myself with experimental fashion and style too. I plundered my mum's shimmery saris and treasure trove of jewellery boxes (an array of chocolate boxes and biscuit tins brimming with golden and plastic delights) and soon began mixing them with vintage European items from my Oma's incredibly chic, understated wardrobe. I sought to make bold multicultural fashion statements, trying to emulate what I saw on my favourite supermodels Yasmeen Ghauri (who I discovered to my delight was mixed Pakistani and German) and Naomi Campbell, whose father is Jamaican and Chinese. My bedroom was plastered with portraits I had drawn of them too, alongside many ripped out pages of them in *Vogue* and *i-D* magazine. Building a sense of my own identity through my multicultural style would eventually lead me to a career as a fashion editor in London.

My dad, who was a photographer himself, took the most wonderful photos of me as a child. Inspired by my special bond with my dad, I learned to enjoy being in front of the camera too! He gave me several cameras so I very soon became an early adopter of the selfie, using my digital camera to take endless photos of myself from various angles. Friends joked I was 'self-obsessed' – remember this was in the late 90s into the 'nasty noughties' where you were susceptible to extreme ridicule if you indulged in self-care or anything to do with celebrating yourself. Now I recognise this also fed into a typical microaggression towards mixed people, where we so often get stereotyped as shallow, when in reality we might be self-exploring for more profound reasons! As it happens many multicultural and mixed artists have tried to make sense of themselves in this way, through studying themselves in self-portraiture – from Frida Kahlo (Indigenous Mexican, Spanish, German and Hungarian-Jewish) to Andy Warhol (American and Polish immigrant ancestry) to Dame Tracey Emin (Turkish-Cypriot and Romany-English) to Sarah Maple (Kenyan, Punjabi and British).

Lynn Ann Searcy, the iconic mixed protagonist from the millennial US sitcom *Girlfriends*, was also permanently on a mission to discover and express herself. Lynn's character was written with a nuance that is still rarely afforded to mixed and multiracial characters on screen. Her complexity and struggles were endearing and added dimension, with storylines of being adopted by white parents and finally meeting her Black father after constant soul searching speaking to a vulnerability beneath her independent, carefree, freaky facade. Aged 17, I got a copyright tattoo on my shoulder as a defiant symbol of my mixed difference, telling my friends it marked my 'uniqueness'. Looking back it was quite the political statement, and I think it's the reason I still like my tattoo today. I look upon it lovingly as quite a Lynn from *Girlfriends* thing to do!

Kyley Winfield is an award-winning leader, higher-education CEO and multidisciplinary artist who I met on the London 'Indie Sleaze' scene in the late 2000s. I was interested to speak to him about his experience as an artist discovering his mixed identity through the club/ music/fashion circuit:

I remember people saying to me, 'Oh, you look like Jimi Hendrix!' And I got to the point where I'd walk down the street and people I didn't know would just shout 'Jimi Hendrix' at me and I found it really annoying!! I felt like... 'I'm an individual!!' But then I started watching Jimi Hendrix videos, and I knew 'Voodoo Child', but I didn't know anything else about him, because it was sort of the days before YouTube was a thing, so I hadn't really had access to him, or how he looked – or how he moved. But I thought he's really cool and I could see it's actually not a bad thing [people were saying that]. I started to feel influenced by him. I felt a really strong connection with Jimi Hendrix, who is also mixed heritage.

Hendrix was someone 'outside the box' who Kyley could connect with: 'He had mixed heritage, and was into shamanism. So I was really feeling that energy. And I was recording with another band, in LA with established artists and music legends – I was feeding off that energy too.'

Kyley noticed he was intuitively pulled towards culturally mixing styles: 'I think I just drew on so many different musical genres, from being in a heavy metal band, and even though I mostly played indie rock music, I was also drawing on probably some of the wildness of heavy metal but then also some of the kind of sensitivity of folk music.'

I remember Kyley for his intensely energetic band antics – like playing his bass upside down and on his head, and then jumping from great heights in his luminous pink skinny jeans, ripped vest and bandana straight into the audience, or climbing up scaffolding at gigs. I wondered if he feels, looking back, whether all this energy helped him release some mixed angst, Rage Against the Machine style (whose lead singer Zack de la Rocha is mixed Chicano, African, Sephardi Jewish, German and Irish whilst the band's founder and lead guitarist Tom Morello is mixed Kenyan, Irish and Italian).

'I have been starting to think about that as well, about how much I danced, how much I needed to move', contemplates Kyley.

I'm sure part of the bright clothing was to be seen for something other than my skin colour – rather than just being the Black guy in the band. I definitely worked through a lot of stuff by performing and just moving my body. I remember playing one of the last Frog nights [iconic London indie night] and the energy just took over my body. I remember just spinning around and just having this huge release!!

When people talk about Jimi Hendrix, they don't say 'Black guitarist, Jimi Hendrix'. You just go, 'Jimi Hendrix'. He's someone that has been described as transcending race. And Slash [the legendary top hat and shades-wearing guitarist from Guns 'n' Roses] said people said, 'Are you Black? Are you white?' And Slash said, 'I want to forget all of that. I'm gonna grow my hair long and just get into rock and roll.'

Selfie sketches:

- Draw, paint, sketch or collage your image (using cut-up magazines).
- Think about how you feel about yourself away from other people's gaze and try to express that, whether in abstract or naturalistic form.

Journal your feelings:

- Write down your thoughts about your face and body to release your emotions. Write poetry or stories about yourself and how you feel about being in a mixed body.

Get inspired!

- Find characters, cartoons and people who bear a resemblance to you phenotypically or whom you relate to and draw or journal about them and why they inspire you.

FEELING DISCONNECTED FROM YOUR MIXED BODY

If the world has been confusing or unwelcoming of our mixed experience, we may unknowingly cut ourselves off from our connection with our mixed body. In turn, we may become disconnected from our own complicated feelings to prevent further pain. This is a very human coping mechanism that happens unconsciously, and it's far more common in the general population than we care to realise. We might do this without noticing, as a way of numbing the complexity of emotions that have nowhere to go.

Allyson Inez Ford, aka the Body Justice Therapist, is a Dutch-Indonesian and Mexican-American clinical psychotherapist based in Southern California who specialises in body issues, OCD, trauma and multicultural identity. She grew up near Seattle in an all-American majority white town which affected her self-image as a mixed child, and she relates her eating disorder to the shame she felt around her mixed identity growing up:

> I remember just feeling kind of embarrassed that my family was different. And I don't know exactly how that started, except for just general messaging about white bodies being preferred. And I remember feeling embarrassed when people would come over to my house and we would have different types of foods than just typical American meals. I wouldn't invite people over much because I was embarrassed.

Allyson was also racially bullied.

> I got on the school bus with my brother and there was a group of popular white kids sitting in the back and they held up this sign that said, 'No burnt tacos past this point!' And I just remember feeling so ashamed and so embarrassed, and that's when my body hatred started. This is also the time just before puberty when my body was already changing, and then I started to feel like being in my skin was not a desired thing or a good thing.

For Allyson, her body shame resulted in a kind of self-erasure of pretending to be monoracial.

> I started really hiding the fact that I was mixed race. I would tell people that I was Hawaiian, because that somehow seemed more acceptable than being part Mexican or part Indonesian. My middle name is Inez but I would tell my people my middle name was Rochelle. I just disconnected from myself so much and that's when eating disorder stuff and body image struggles started, where I'd try to shrink my body to be more like my white peers' boyish frame – very thin – it was like me trying to assimilate. It took moving away from that area to work on a sense of acceptance.

> Now I live in Southern California and there's tons of different ethnicities

around me, and it's more accepted to be of a different race or multiracial here. It took a long time finding my own mixed race community to undo some of that body hate, and to recover from eating disorder stuff. That's why I wanted to be a therapist, because I was going through my own eating disorder recovery and discussion around race and certainly multiracial experience was completely left out of eating disorder treatment!

Therapist and author Reesma Menekem specialises in the relationship between trauma and what he calls 'white body supremacy' – his concept being that we need to focus on the *language of bodies* because 'white bodies are seen to be dominant' i.e. seen as the standard or more preferable to BIPOC bodies and it's our bodies that hold onto the trauma. Reesma uses the term 'bodies of culture' to convey that non-white bodies have to manage themselves within the pressures of white supremacy. This might be affecting BIPOC and mixed people in a way mainstream medical treatment hasn't recognised. Eating disorders are so often seen as a 'white body' issue, but in 2021 *The Guardian* newspaper reported that 'The number of hospital admissions for eating disorders is rising at a faster rate among people from ethnic minorities in England, prompting concerns that there may be cultural or racial factors driving them.'[4] And UK eating disorder charity Beat say 'What the limited research *does* show is Black teenagers are 50% more likely than white teenagers to exhibit binge and purge behaviours (Goeree, Sovinsky, & Iorio, 2011). And a recent NHS report revealed that between 2017–2020, there was a 216% increase in the number of Black people admitted to hospital because of an eating disorder.'[5]

Western medical treatment predominantly focuses on the mind *dominating* the body rather than utilising the useful somatic information that arises through emotions and feelings inside our bodies, but a revolution in trauma therapy over the past 30 years means trauma experts like Bessel Van der Kolk, who wrote the best-selling book *The Body Keeps the Score*, and Gabor Maté, who wrote *When the Body Says No*, have changed how we think about the link between trauma and the body – and this relates to being BIPOC and mixed too. Through this trauma lens Allyson's 'mixed body of culture' needed a way of trying to escape a mixed identity she didn't understand and therefore felt shameful of. Allyson is also the child of multigenerationally mixed parents and is aware of the generational trauma 'legacies' (see Chapter 2) from her Mexican and Indonesian ancestral lines that might affect her body too.

Somatic awareness is where we can listen into our body's wisdom by getting in touch with internal sensations such as pain, tingling, temperature, etc. to reflect and discover what it might be trying to tell us about our well-being. Allyson remarkably used her body and mind intelligence together to understand what was happening to her:

I started reading about multiracial experiences and sort of connecting the dots around my own eating disorder and body image stuff and how it related to being multiracial – just feeling like you never really belong, feeling like you're never really good enough. And our bodies are objectified and always exoticised.

Like many women of colour Allyson found herself catcalled and sexualised by men at a young age:

A part of me felt like it was finally sort of seen in a 'positive' way. I started seeking male attention through that, but inside, it didn't feel good. And it didn't help me really develop a sense of self-worth. It was just still like my body being objectified in a different way, and seeing me for my body and not who I am, again, this message of, like, your body's the problem!

BEING RACIALLY FETISHISED

Fetishisation is the dehumanising act of objectifying someone and desiring them based on an aspect of their identity. This happens a lot to BIPOC people but particularly to Black women and men, East Asian women, and indigenous and Latino people who all often end up being cast as sexual props in the lives of those who exotify and *other* them.

Racial tropes are recurrent archetypal themes that appear over and over again throughout culture, occurring in films and other storytelling narratives. Some tropes used in racial fetishisation include negative caricatures like The Jezebel and The Mandigo, a racist narrative that Black women and men are 'hyper-sexual' and 'animalistic', born from colonisation and the Jim Crow slavery era where dehumanising Black people helped legitimise the harm being caused to them by white slavers. Other examples include the Asian Hooker, based on Chinese, Filipina and Korean 'comfort women' – enslaved women and sex workers used by military serviceman in World War 2; the China Doll or 'Lotus

Flower' – a submissive hyper-feminine Asian female whose subservient role depicts the West's dominance over the East; and the Spicy Latina – who is hyper-sexual, hot-tempered and aggressive, based on stereotypes that Latinos are 'wild, dangerous and untrustworthy', making them scapegoats for illegal immigration, crime and unemployment in America.

Racist tropes feed into unconscious issues around fear and wanting to dominate the *other* in a bid to gain control over the unknown. Mixed and multiracial people are also susceptible to being racially and sexually fetishised, because we are seen as exotic in comparison to *everyone* else. This 'rare bird' trope conjures up a kind of 'genetic limited edition' desirability from outsiders where the mixed person is projected with other people's fantasies of envy and fascination that they must be self-obsessed and narcissistic, constantly thinking about how they look. By far the most historically used racist trope about mixed people is the 'Tragic Mulatto' who is very often beautiful and 'rare' but doomed to terrible life circumstances because of being born as – *shock, horror* – mixed race! The tragic mulatto was a common trope in post-slavery-era American cinema in films like *Imitation of Life* (1934) and *Pinky* (1949) that told us tragedy was our multiracial destiny because... *imagine being nearly white, but not quite!* How horrific that must be for us! This pitiful gaze on mixed people served white audiences who felt sympathetic to tragic mulatto storylines.

MIXED BEAUTY OBSESSION

The fixation with 'mixed beauty' from the late 2010s to the 2020s is something that we will hopefully look back on in years to come more objectively as problematic in many ways. Never has racial ambiguity and looking mixed race been more fashionable and aspirational, with many using tanning, styling and cosmetic procedures to achieve a slightly 'more ethnic' look. Natalie Morris, author of *Mixed/Other*, wrote the article 'Why celebrating "mixed-race beauty" has its problematic side' in *The Guardian* and warned that we should 'push back against this disproportionate interest in how we look'. She goes on to discuss how historically this kind of polarisation has always been dangerous for us:

It wasn't so long ago that the mixed population was being scrutinised with a similar energy but with an entirely different outcome. In the 1930s and 1940s, there were groups warning about the dangers of 'race crossing'; there were calls for mixed people to be sterilised; we were denigrated as deviant, stupid, contaminated, undesirable. Isn't the contemporary idealisation of mixedness – the suggestion that we are more beautiful or have 'the best of both' – simply the other side of the same coin?[6]

The overarching influence of celebrity icon Kim Kardashian, herself of Armenian and white American (as well as purportedly Scottish, Dutch, English, Irish) descent, has impressively shifted the beauty standard from white, skinny and blonde towards dark, ethnically ambiguous and curvaceous (though how long this trend will last is debatable). Interestingly, Kardashian's own ethnicity origin backstory *also* reflects the cultural shapeshifting she is so renowned for; given her Middle Eastern and white heritage, many would describe Kardashian as 'mixed race' although she self-describes as white. This is likely because Armenians who emigrated to America fought to classify themselves as white in the *United States vs Cartozian* case when Armenians officially became white in 1924.

Kardashian's uncanny ability to generate cultural controversy and capitalise on this by cosplaying various ethnic presentations with styling and alleged surgeries means she constantly receives accusations of 'Blackfishing' (where makeup, styling and/or bodily enhancements are used to appear Black). In 2018 she wore her hair in *Fulani* braids (a traditional West African hairstyle) and credited them to Bo Derek, a white woman. And she has also been accused of cultural appropriation by the South Asian community for repeatedly wearing a *Maang tikka* (a traditional style of South Asian jewellery). The Kardashian aesthetic influence is indisputably omnipresent but whether it has helped or hindered BIPOC and mixed people is full of ambiguity. The look certainly inspires many to emulate the 'racially/ethnically ambiguous look' like a costume from the fancy dress store. Some white women fake tan evermore drastically and dye their hair jet black, filling their eyebrows in so heavily that many of us who might have once been shunned for having a 'naturally Kardashian look' have started to look *white* in comparison to white women who cosplay as mixed and BIPOC.

'I have been asked what fake tan I use, and one time faced confusion from a white person who couldn't believe that my entire body was the same colour, leaving me blankly staring back and trying to work out if they were joking', says Laila Woozeer in *The Metro* newspaper. Not only is it bizarre for BIPOC people to experience not being believed that our actual skin is our *natural* colour, but the entire perception of 'tanning' itself is another problematic area, where as mixed people, our skin naturally switching in summertime might be mistaken for a fake tan by others without them realising how tone deaf that is.

Actress and filmmaker Rashida Jones, who is of Cameroonian, Welsh, Ashkenazi Jewish and Russian American heritage, was told by an interviewer at TNT's 2015 SAG Awards, 'You look amazing, gorgeous! You look like you have just come off a tropical island or something. You're very tan, very tropical.' Rashida's deadpan response, 'I mean, you know I'm ethnic,' went viral and was thoroughly appreciated by many frustrated fellow mixed and multiracial people.

Drastically transforming into a whole different shade with the first hint of sunshine is something that happens to mixed and multiracial people naturally and it's not a decision we make to beautify ourselves, but rather just nature taking its course. I easily metamorphose from a pallid yellowy-white tone reminiscent of Dracula in winter to a deep reddish brown a la Princess Jasmine in the summer, and it only takes me a couple of hours. What happens to our mixed skin is not really a 'tan' in the same way white people often purchase a tan or try to tan, but rather I think of it as our chameleon-like melanin awakening!

Similarly to being in awe of a 'tan', some white people also aspire to having certain phenotypically Black or brown features and traits without respecting or understanding the struggle that comes with living in a BIPOC body under white supremacy. Some features are currently coveted, e.g. big lips, curvy hips and bums, whilst others, like prominent noses, are still seen as 'too ethnic'. When model Bella Hadid (Palestinian and Dutch American) expressed regret for getting plastic surgery to reshape her 'ethnic' nose, she heartbreakingly told *Vogue* magazine that she wished she had kept her 'ancestors' nose' and it made her feel disconnected from her Arab relatives.

Children are being affected by mixed beauty obsession as well. Many adults flock to mixed race baby Instagram accounts to salivate over the desirable mixed features of some poor child who has been turned into an exotic trophy. Likes and gushing comments raise the social currency of a parent who benefits vicariously from the coveted mixed phenotype of their child. A white parent with low self-esteem about their own appearance might gain significantly in this way by capitalising on the cultural cachet of a mixed child who becomes an object of envy and desire that boosts their own personal status. Rather than being flattering to mixed people who witness this, it feels fetishistic and exploitative, akin to animals being observed in a zoo.

Jumping on the mixed beauty bandwagon, the British tabloid newspapers seem to have developed a vested interest because stirring racial tensions between mixed and non-mixed people of colour is effective clickbait. Divisive headlines like 'Why mixed people are seen as more attractive' create discord by triggering self-worth issues on all sides. I know I'm not alone in how this kind of thing makes me wince, watching how it insidiously dehumanises us, whilst also perpetuating division within our own communities by reinforcing the stereotype that mixed people are a monolith who all find ourselves more attractive than monoracial people. This is actually based on yet another stereotypical trope of the 'vacuous, self-obsessed' mixed person who only cares about their looks. It's also worth reflecting on how our proximity to whiteness as the beauty ideal is what usually makes 'mixed race beauty' so desirable. Whiteness is upheld by society as a code for 'better', 'aspirational', 'expensive', 'pure', 'higher quality', etc. so when you are mixed, whiteness provides a certain prestige regardless of whether someone is attractive or not.

I've had to grapple with what I can only describe as the *uncomfortable awe* that my mum has displayed towards traits of mine that she considers whiter. Compliments like 'You are so tall and stunning!! Not like me, short and fat!' were generously intended but instead made me feel icky and annoyed that she was putting herself down in order to validate me. Far from helping raise my mixed self-esteem, Mum constantly pointing out how I didn't look like her, implying I looked better than her due to my proximity to whiteness, was painful and alienating. A child doesn't want their parent to admire them like an object in the British museum, in an *othering* way. I simply wanted to look like my beautiful mum (who is very beautiful in her own right, I might add!) so that I could feel connected to her as her child.

MIXED MALE BODIES

We hear a lot from women about the attention we receive for our looks and the fetishisation we face, but we hear less from men, particularly

COMING HOME TO YOUR MIXED BODY

cisgender men. This is because within a patriarchy men are assigned dominant social roles, and there's stigma attached to complaining about attention from the opposite sex, even when their experience is negative. Mixed and multiracial men, particularly Black mixed men, are often stereotyped as 'softer' (i.e. less 'Black') and their beauty might cause them to be aligned with emasculating qualities like femininity, which is perceived at being at odds with the trope of 'strong Black man' – which they are *also* expected to live up to in a kind of double bind, where they are damned if they do and damned if they don't.

Actor Albert Magashi, who is of Tanzanian and Bulgarian mixed heritage, stars in the play *For Black Boys Who Have Considered Suicide When the Hue Gets Too Heavy*. He says in an interview with *Mixed Messages*, a weekly newsletter that focuses on mixed race experiences, that his character Sable is 'the only mixed-race slash lightskin character in "For Black Boys". It's definitely a conversation.' *Mixed Messages* then asks, 'Have you noticed any stereotypes around mixedness? How do you want this conversation to develop?' To which Albert responds, 'The stereotype for mixed race guys is that they are like...', to which *Mixed Messages* offers 'Fuckboys?', to which Albert replies, 'Exactly that'.[7]

As a therapist, Alex Lewis (who you met in Chapter 2) is concerned about how mixed men can build their self-esteem if so much of their worth is based on their looks and attractiveness.

In terms of being fetishised, 'the negative is at a young age it feeds into our need for approval, love and acceptance', he explains, 'so if our entire self-worth is then tied up with us being mixed race – then that feeds into the need for constant external validation.'

So how does Alex feel about harmful tropes directed specifically at Black mixed men, in particular those so often found in social media commentary when discussing the TV show *Love Island*? 'In terms of the stereotype of the mixed raced man being a "player" – men could be in danger of believing they are not worth much more than their looks,' he offers.

This serves as something which benefits young men who are looking for a place to belong, but over time this external need for approval will no longer serve them as it has in the past because they get to know themselves and realise that it doesn't quite fulfil them as much.

I truly believe in all instances, but in particular with people who struggle with their identity, there is the danger of leaning into the stereotypes of any particular race, e.g. being 'Black and dangerous' is seen as something to be proud of as people are less likely to attack you. Or by being seen as a 'player' and fetishised, although a negative thing, it serves young men in getting what they want. I'm sure if a mixed ethnicity child felt like they were accepted for who they are it is less likely they would feel the need to adhere to the stereotypes which are so commonly associated with them.

Being racially fetishised might look like:

- Noticing your white partner only dates mixed people or people of colour. Or your monoracial partner of colour only dates mixed or light-skinned people.
- Compliments feeling more like racial exotification or an obsession with your skin tone or features than anything about you personally as a human being.
- Being told by a white person that they want to try out a Black/brown person and you're not 'fully' Black/brown so they feel 'more comfortable' with you.
- An underlying feeling that your partner more often than not makes you feel like a sexual object, or a trophy.

CONNECTING WITH YOUR MIXED RACE HAIR

As well as struggling with their looks and bodies, I have witnessed so many harrowing stories from my Black mixed clients about their hair struggles, and trying to build relationships with their hair, when parents and caregivers have not known how to care for it.

British Black mixed Jamaican musician and artist FKA Twigs told *The Face* magazine how she and her Spanish mum learnt how to do her hair when they went to a show in London and met another mixed girl and her mum in the toilet queue, who gave them some great advice: 'I remember my mum asking the mum how to do my hair – this other girl had really, really beautiful hair.'[8] But when FKA Twigs and her mum tried it out themselves, her friends from school in Gloucestershire were bullying and dismissive. 'They used to call me Barnett – and they were like: "Eugh, Barnett, your hair's so greasy!" And I remember them touching my plaits and all the grease coming off, and saying: "Oh my God it's so greasy!"' Here FKA Twigs recounts the trauma of finally finding a solution, but then also having to deal with the aftermath of being othered for that, as well.

Jamila Andersson, a Filipino-Nigerian transpersonal psychotherapist, shares how her hair journey has also been one of constant challenge, reflection and self-healing. 'For almost 20 years, I never knew what my hair texture looked like naturally,' Jamila begins. 'I internalised the belief that something was wrong with my hair, which also affected my perception of myself. Something was wrong with me, because my hair could not fit in with any group.'

> I found a hair salon that would straighten my hair with chemical relaxers. It became an obsession for me to have the perfect straight hair. I realise now that my obsession was about control; I could control how my hair looked and, by extension, how others perceived me. This need stemmed from needing more understanding and acceptance of my natural hair texture. I needed to learn about what my hair texture required but back then straight hair was the only option. In the 2000s it was cool to have the 'Rachel from Friends' haircut but it was very damaging to my scalp and hair. The chemicals used in the straightening process altered the structure of my hair and caused significant damage to my scalp, leading to hair loss and other issues. I judged my hair harshly as 'challenging to handle', wishing I had my mother's Filipino hair.

Thankfully Jamila found her way to her embracing her natural hair texture and she now supports others on their hair journey.

> Ultimately, embracing mixed race hair is a powerful affirmation of identity and a celebration of the richness that comes from cultural fusion. Mixed-race hair textures defy simplistic classification; they are fluid and evolving, reflecting the diversity inherent in their owners. This fluidity challenges societal norms that seek to confine individuals to neat categories, encouraging acceptance of complexity and change.

Jamila speaks more about her hair in Chapter 6 and you can learn her tips on hair self-care in her transpersonal hair diary exercise in Chapter 12.

HONOURING YOUR MIXED BODY THROUGH MOVEMENT, DANCE AND YOGA

After trying yoga for many years in various spaces and never feeling quite right, I eventually found solace for my multiracial body in Rajbir Singh's classes. As a British-born Indian Sikh yoga instructor, Rajbir naturally embraces elements of *Sanatana Dharma*, the ancient spiritual wisdom behind yoga. With its focus on service, meditation and spirituality, Rajbir's teachings finally connected me with my South Asian roots through *Pranayama* (a traditional Yogic breathing technique to enhance vitality) and *mantra* (sacred words or syllables repeated to help spiritual transformation). This naturally helped my mixed body feel more like home in an authentic way. I also noticed that his brilliant classes attracted many BIPOC people because he emphasises body safety awareness, especially for Black and brown bodies of culture – which is also how I met Anne Shalo, a Cameroonian and American UK-based yoga instructor, sound healer and 'Divine Dance' facilitator. Anne's transpersonal classes incorporate sound and movement together, often bringing elements of *Kemetic* yoga (African/Egyptian yoga) and traditional *Hatha* yoga through sound bowls and shamanic chanting from her Cameroonian ancestry.

Anne was raised in Oak Park, Illinois in a town that prided itself on its diversity. She grew up 'half Black, but not African-American half Black', with a white mother originally from Michigan. 'I was African Black', says Anne, pointing out an important distinction in the US, as she started to realise that even as a mixed person she was still culturally different to her mixed peers. 'As I started to get older, I started to think, like, Hmm, where is my space?' says Anne.

Anne was a part of a dance company from a young age, which helped her in many ways.

It was really powerful, and I became so aware of my connection to my body, but because of the toxicity within the dance realm, and white bodies being mainly what you see, especially in the ballet world, there was an extra level of judgement, and a higher expectation for myself was born. I felt I had to do better because my body didn't fit. I had to go above and beyond so there was that pressure, and I don't think it was something really conscious, probably until I was in my teenage years.

Eventually Anne started to realise the harm being perpetuated around her Black mixed body.

As my body started to change, I became more aware of my own self-image. And it is quite damaging, in dance class, when there's a person that's pointed out for having good technique or doing something right, and then they're put on a pedestal, and then you compare yourself to that. Your improvements and your goals and everything are based on that person achieving something in somebody else's body, that actually may not be physically possible within yourself.

A realisation that Anne's self-worth was being devastated by the lack of representation in the field finally hit home. 'It wasn't until my twenties, when I studied dance at university, that I started to realise that I didn't love it any more. I was doing it just for external validation; I'd given away all of my worth to somebody else, for their judgement and validation.' The racial and psychological elements were too much to bear and affected Anne's mental health.

Ballet is renowned for being quite racist and very white body focused, and not making it through to the final round was like the end of the world. And doing that time and time again, it definitely develops your perseverance and toughness – but then how far do you let it go? It was taking a toll on my mental health, and I just realised, I hated my body and there was nothing that I could say that was nice about myself.

So Anne started to reconsider her proximity to whiteness within this context. 'I think because I was so familiar with being around white people and the white standard, from having a white mom, there was a bit of an illusion before I realised it.' She then found a role model: 'I think Misty Copeland was the first ballet dancer to come out and have a platform for, like, mixed race dancers, and then, in turn, the Black ballerina. But that was what, maybe nine years ago. But up until that point, it wasn't really a conversation!!'

Slowly but surely, Anne started to reclaim her body on her own terms.

For my body in particular, it got to a point where I'd realised I couldn't compare myself to anybody else, because my body was a mixture of things. With that self-awareness I gained, that I do have a choice, and I don't have to fit a mould, or, you know, change, depending on who I'm around. At the same time, I can actually feel into what it means to be mixed, to feel like, what does my body need? What is the story within me?

Unity of self was Anne's goal. 'Marrying the mind and the body were at the forefront of my healing journey. It's like there's this grounding, just kind of opening and an expansion that takes place. And almost with that expansion, you realise you're limitless, and you CAN take up space, because you are literally stepping into your space no matter what shape you are!' She says powerfully: 'No matter what colour, or even if it's different to everybody else's, you can take your space unapologetically!'

REFLECTION

1. What is your relationship to your mixed body – do you feel connected or disconnected? Think about incorporating your hair, features and skin tone when reflecting on this.
2. Think back to how you felt about your mixed body growing up and compare that to yourself as an adult. Has there been a change or have your feelings stayed the same?
3. Take three deep breaths and bring your attention within for a few moments. What can you notice or feel about your body? Write down what comes up and if there is nothing, that's OK, just gently notice without judgement.

Chapter 4

Freeing your mixed voice

RELEASING FEAR + OPENING UP

It's hard being British, especially when you're Brit-ish,
three generations deep,
and people still ask where I'm from,
and I normally say Britain,
but maybe I'm wrong, because I know
I'm a little bit Scottish and maybe a little bit Greek.
My grandparents came from Jamaica,
but my granddaddy looked like a Sikh

'HALF-STEREOTYPE', LUKE AG

We ALL have a voice inside of us – our own unique sound of multi-racial expression that is yearning to be heard in all its truth, substance and glory. Our personal mixed voice might be stifled or particularly difficult to connect with, because of all the numerous ways we have been expected to shut ourselves down over the years. We may not even know our voice is *there*, what it even sounds like, or what we actually *want* to say about being mixed...

By saying this I am not recommending you should publicly rush out and make a big announcement about your identity, especially before you feel ready. Rather, this is about gently exploring the unique expression your soul is calling for you to convey in your own world regarding your mixedness. Wouldn't it be *powerful* to be able to feel more comfortable about speaking out what you know to be true about the content of your mixed experiences to your peers – to express what really happens in your family, at school, university or at work, and to eventually have the language to explain to others how you could be better supported and *seen* by them? There will be parts of your mixedness that you have squashed down to appease others without ever even realising. And there are very likely things you really need to say to someone, but that you hide, even from yourself, because it's so hard to explain. Imagine how it would it feel to tell your own mixed story without holding anything back?

Although we might not share exactly the same experiences, so many people of marginalised, discriminated identities also find it challenging to connect with their voice and to speak up. When I need inspiration to connect with my inner truth, I often think of the queer Black feminist and professor Audre Lorde, who courageously wrote: 'My silences had not protected me. Your silence will not protect you. What are the words you do not have yet? What do you need to say?'[1]

Authentic expression comes from *deep* within. The more we connect with our own unique internal world through deciphering the somatic information from how we feel in our bodies, the more we will develop the tools to *hear* our *real* voice. We do this by travelling inwards – close your eyes for a moment and take three deep breaths. Place one hand on your heart whilst you think about your own mixed experience – because this communication needs to come from *your* heart. It's sometimes helpful to do this at night when you are lying in bed with the lights off so that you can experience your own vulnerability. Take a moment to deeply listen into and *attune* to your innermost self and its messages about your multiracial experience.

Breathe it

Breathe deeply into your heart a few times and breathe out any grief or sadness that comes up. You might like to imagine yourself breathing in courage and breathing out fear. Deep inner listening involves focusing on the breath to intuit the messages your body is trying to convey.

Allow it

What does your body and the journey it has been on (think about what we explored last chapter) really want to say if it could speak? Imagine talking candidly and authentically from your heart about being mixed with no self-policing. Whereabouts in your body is the permission to say this – is there one particular area, like your stomach or your chest, where you are noticing sensations?

Feel it

There are no incorrect emotions – if you feel a sense of joy and gratitude about your mixed identity, breathe into that. If you feel some difficult feelings like frustration or anger, notice that too and continue to breathe into them, allowing any tears if they arise.

Speak it

Speak out or note down any words that arise about your mixedness and don't worry if they don't make perfect sense or full sentences right now – this is more about feeling your way towards your voice via your body. Whatever arises is valid – whether a sound or a word. If nothing comes, that's OK too – simply continue this practice exploring what eventually comes up.

LOST ASPECTS OF MIXED SELFHOOD

There are so many highly specific reasons why we might be, unknowingly in some cases, full of pent-up sadness for lost experiences of when we had to shapeshift ourselves to fit a prescribed racial mould, and how, looking back, that might feel painful. Not having ever had a community to share our feelings with, parents to support us or the language to explain, or not knowing at the time how to stand up for our mixed identity, might be festering inside us without an outlet for release.

Lydia Puricelli, who you met in Chapter 1, feels sad about not being able to connect with her family, due to not knowing her 'mother tongue'. Though some of us may be bilingual or multilingual, being unable to access any of our languages is common for many mixed people (myself included!) and can create resistance around connecting with your inner voice. Lydia says:

I feel myself getting quite emotional as I say this, I feel a lump in my throat because at times I feel very disconnected from my family. My voice is breaking now because the thing that I am supposed to be ethnically the most of – because my mum is Indian Punjabi – I've had the least amount of exposure to, and I feel an immense sense of of loss about growing up where my brother and me would be sitting at my grandparents' or my uncle's house and everyone was talking in Punjabi or Hindi. And my cousins, aunts, uncles, everyone would be talking together, but we couldn't speak the language or understand anything.

Create your own mixed + multiracial grief ritual

Letting go can greatly clear the old residue of the past, to make way for new authentic experiences and more integrated self-expression.

- Choose a meaningful object connected to your mixed experience – it could be something culturally symbolic or even a photo that evokes specific memories.
- Place the object in your safe space and light a candle next to it to symbolise your sacred connection to it.
- Sit with the object in stillness for extended and repeated periods, taking time to connect with your breath and feeling any emotion that comes up.
- Extinguish the candle whenever you feel called, to mark the end of your grief ritual, and repeat when necessary until you begin to feel relief.

OPENING UP TO INNER EXPRESSION

Often we will easily dismiss our own inner voice, or are harshly judgemental and critical about it because we may have been taught through society or family that what we think and feel about our mixed identity is invalid or irrelevant. But quite the opposite becomes available to you when you authentically use your voice for healing and connecting with your true self.

Jasmin Harsono is a sound practitioner who works with sound and the voice to help people connect with their inner expression in everyday life. She was born in London and describes herself as 'British' but 'ethnically as Iranian, Welsh and Italian'. Jasmin 'sounds' her voice for her own practice, because she understands how restricting it is for your mixed voice to go unheard.

'My journey from a young age has been that I've felt shut down in sharing my voice about my lived experiences,' says Jasmin.

> *People around me have spoken over me or shut down my opinions and I found it really hard to use my speaking voice. I've always loved to sing and it was always a release, whether it's singing songs or humming to birdsong. I've always felt like [using my voice] was able to immediately take me to my safe space.*

Mixed and multiracial nervous systems might be conditioned to a state of fight, flight, freeze or fawn trauma response. Humming is clinically proven to help soothe a dysregulated nervous system because it calms the vagus nerve (the longest nerve in the central autonomic nervous system), so Jasmin's approach is a *direct* way to support nervous system regulation.

Jasmin harnesses the voice to work through feelings that come up for her around her mixed identity.

> *If I'm finding it hard to process something, 'sounding' my voice helps to release tension and bring awareness and release to the emotion or issue. My voice has become a portal with spirit coming through me – it's intuitive. I don't even need to describe anything in words – it's just the sound for me. It's the ultimate medicine and therapy and that has really helped me.*

When Jasmin was suffering from depression, voice work supported her recovery. 'When I'm feeling low and sometimes you just don't want to do anything, if I started humming it felt like such a breakthrough. It softens everything and you start to feel like "you" again. This is the way that voice practice can really be groundbreaking for people, especially for mixed, people suffering who may not have the words a lot of the time to be able to explain what they're experiencing,' she advises.

I think, for anyone who doesn't have a voice or hasn't been given a voice, it's just incredible because you open up to your true voice – the truth of 'your sound'. It can be messy – it doesn't have to sound beautiful!! That's the whole point of the sound – it's releasing inner voices. You're the sound in whatever comes through. You're expressing through sound vibration, spirit, heart, and your body is fully opening and it's not neck up – it's neck down. You're singing from your roots!!

HEALING WITH MUSIC AND SINGING

The first single I ever bought was *Vision of Love* by Mariah Carey in 1992, but I was too young to know that Mariah was mixed back then. All I knew was that the expansive qualities of her voice deeply resonated with my soul to the point I would play and rewind the cassette over and over until it got worn out! I had never heard someone sing like that before! Through her incredible voice Mariah spans the deepest depths and the highest heights of human expression, something right between an opera singer and a classic soul superstar channelling her mixedness into pure transcendental sound and energy. Little did I know, Mariah had brought the magic of mixed expression directly to my door. We can't all be on that level of craftsmanship, but what I'm trying to show you is that Mariah discovered how to connect with herself and her voice so deeply that she opened up a whole world. If you read her life story you will appreciate why she strived so hard to do that, as an escape – creating new worlds with themes of fantasy and love, when she has also struggled so much in her family background and mixed experience. Much like the mantra we discussed in the last chapter, many of Mariah's song lyrics read like self-affirmations for mixedness too!

Singing along to your favourite songs (without self-judgement!) as a means of connecting with the joy of self-expression is a wonderfully playful way to explore your feelings about being mixed, particularly feelings of grief and sadness. Music also gives you a chance to listen to other people's perspectives and to learn how they choose to express themselves differently from you, and from each other. Of course music is created by all races of artists for us to feel divinely connected to, because music, like all creative expression, transcends race, but listening to mixed artists in particular can help provide and open up insight and understanding.

Here is a playlist of songs from my mixed playlist, by various mixed and multiracial artists. Some are explicitly about being mixed, and others might simply have a feeling that I can connect to in the unspoken expression of their mixedness. You can make your own interpretations as you wish and hopefully you will feel inspired to create your own mixed playlist. Here are a few tracks to get you started:

Mixed playlist

- 'Gotta Work' – Amerie
- 'Hafu' – Maia Borough
- 'Hard Out Here' – Raye
- 'One Love' – Bob Marley
- 'The Lighthouse' – Halsey
- 'Apple' – Charli XCX
- 'Identity' – X Ray Spex
- 'Georgetown' – Loyle Carner ft John Agard
- 'Young Fresh and New' – Kelis
- 'Fear of a Mixed Planet' – Shock G
- 'Mixed Feelings' – Logic
- 'Outside' – Mariah Carey
- 'Mooo!' – Doja Cat
- 'What a Feeling' – Irene Cara
- 'Hell Is Round the Corner' – Tricky, Marina Topley-Bird
- 'Cellophane' – FKA Twigs
- 'Blaxican' – M.E.D
- 'Metis(se)' – Yannick Noah ft Disiz
- 'Mixed Race Identity Crisis' – Aaron Glitch
- 'Split' – NIKI

JOURNALING, POETRY AND SPOKEN WORD

One of the best ways to work out what you really want to say is to journal. Using a free writing approach where you simply 'word vomit' onto the page without editing or stopping until you feel finished can help people who don't want to speak everything out loud to still have a voice. Aiming to be non-judgmental about what comes out can feel safe and soothing. You can even rip out what you wrote and throw it in the bin, or burn what you've written afterwards in a cleansing ritual if it feels difficult or too personal. That way, it's just between you and the page.

If you struggle to be honest with yourself, even when no one else can see what you are writing, this will tell you a lot about yourself and what is difficult to say. You can practise trying to be authentic in this new way in private. Writing poetry might be something else you might enjoy as you begin to develop your voice. There are no rules for how to do this and it's always best you do what feels right for you. I have often written poetry for myself, just to get my ideas down. It's not about judging what comes out or showing anyone, but more about learning to be with the truth of what you are feeling, which if you've been shut down for an extensive period of time is a huge achievement in itself!

Luke AG is a Black mixed poet and strategy director, who grew up in Hastings with an English mum and Jamaican father and is now based in New York. Luke wasn't drawn to performing as an entertainer like his mum and dad (who were in legendary 80s dance troupe Hot Gossip). 'I didn't enjoy dancing, I preferred football,' Luke reminisces. Finding his voice through poetry – and notably with his seminal poem on mixed identity, 'Half-Stereotype' – Luke cuts straight to the essence of mixed identity with an expansive thoughtfulness that is sometimes missed in existing mixed storytelling narratives. In his video published online for Metro newspaper, self-assuredness and comfortability with his inner explorations are meticulously woven together in fluid forms, as he strolls through a park.[2]

'Half-Stereotype' went viral and completely blew up after Luke was spotted performing at an open mic night by *The Metro* newspaper, who then asked him to make a video performing his piece. Although it brought him plenty of acclaim, Luke recognises he also felt confused about how performing his mixed race poem made him feel in certain contexts.

Luke: I started getting loads of bookings, and when I was performing it originally in South London clubs, it kind of made sense. But when the audience started changing and then it got to a couple of brands which were like, 'can you do that mixed race poem??' – it was weird.

Namalee: It sounds like you were in danger of becoming a bit of a 'token' – like 'the mixed race poet' 'helping' brands get seen as 'anti-racist'?

Luke: Yeah – every mixed person knows about the fetishisation of our identity and it's something I really struggle with – especially when you're performing something that's trauma. Naturally it becomes something else, something uncomfortable, so it was a weird kind of transition – getting paid by brands but noticing they are not really listening. But they like the 'activism' aspect. It kind of messed me up a bit. It was really cool that it was popular, but I think when things enter public spaces without your control, it can get a bit weird.

Namalee: I can see how that could easily happen – especially with going viral – it's like having an instant audience and it isn't always what we need, as mixed people, as we have so few safe spaces to develop our identity. Like on TikTok for example, there are lots of jokes about mixed race poets and that must be quite disheartening for young people who are just getting started. What are your thoughts on that?

Luke: I do find it interesting why poetry is the vehicle for us. I actually think it's because of the literature that, particularly, a certain generation of people grew up with in school in the UK. Like hearing stuff like Benjamin Zephaniah, and 'Half-Caste' by John Agard. The only experience of ANY mixed conversation was through the lens of poetry in school. And I actually think that subconsciously, it's the only place I've ever thought about identity and therefore became the only 'safe place' where I felt like conversations about it could happen.

Namalee: That is such a good point!! What's hard though is that I don't know how much poets get to actually develop their voice in safety on social media because there's so much ridicule about the 'mixed race experience' so some people get put off I think. What do you feel about social media poetry in general?

Luke: That particular spoken word style often talks about something that might be difficult to talk about, or something they don't really understand yet. And they do it in that 'style' because it's what they have been taught, or seen on socials.

Luke is conscious of the pressures of the fast-paced ever-changing social media landscape:

I think maybe, the thing that was fortunate for me, is that I never watched anyone else do mixed poetry on socials. I was just working in a bar in Hastings, and just felt a need to perform what I felt. I found my therapy on stage because that was a space I could actually talk about it. You can't cure anything, right? But you can practise over and over, and I actually do feel like I am very comfortable with my identity now.

As much as he values his identity, Luke is also keen to avoid being typecast as 'the mixed race poet' because he is aware that can be limiting to his whole identity too. He's ready to move on now:

Luke: I will never get on stage with 'Half-Stereotype' again because I feel like I exorcised it out!! And I think a lot of people are unable, or don't feel like they have the spaces, to exorcise that voice, but you need it to be a safe space – I think it's very necessary. And I think the whole phenomenon of the mixed race poet comes from the need to express something [that's unspoken].

Namalee: Do you have any tips for mixed poets or writers and speakers who really want to talk about their experience?

Luke: My advice is your voice and your performance shouldn't necessarily be for everyone. I think understanding the question of 'why' you're performing: who you're performing to, to understand the intention of the people in the crowd, is very, very TikTok. But you have no control over the audience. You cannot control them. Your stuff just gets taken out of context. And I actually would encourage people to BUILD their voice and get to know the audience they are performing to first. And that's not necessarily to say, 'Oh, you have to go to the venue.' I think it's more considering the spaces you put your poetry into.

Not many people are able to communicate this kind of language, so exposing yourself to people who cannot fundamentally understand what you are talking about and realising that even a lot of 'smart' people don't have the emotional intelligence to understand the need for poetry!! So you have to be careful! You have to be conscious that you can find your voice. Even by starting to speak, like just start doing it in your home – in the shower!!

A lot of the time, people might see someone [else] performing and feel like, 'Oh my God' and feel so removed from maybe how to even begin themselves. So I think – just do it. Just speak it, or sing in the shower. Whatever you want to do! It's just you and your voice. Not writing for an audience was a privilege for me!! Reflecting alone in the shower, in a solo environment, where, ultimately the echo is great too!!

Namalee: That feels a lot 'safer' to me. And it's also fun to practise in the shower!! The audience on social media, more often than not, doesn't always give you the immediate warmth that you feel in the shower, that you need to start off, to feel protected. All of those things are so important, aren't they? Because you're contained in a safe space, you're being nourished by the water!

Luke: And we really need that. It's almost like everybody needs to go in the shower and do that!!

Namalee: I'm really hearing from you, to go inwards, rather than going outwards without having the identity stability yet. And I think if you go inwards, even for me as a mixed therapist, it's like you build the ground within yourself so that when you go back out again, then you know when you're ready to do that. Rather than you vulnerably rushing out, before you've found your voice properly, and you are not in control.

Luke: To be, like, a John Agard – for your poetry to really change the [mixed] narrative, it takes time and a certain degree of [inner strength]. I don't think most 22-year-olds will have that immediately and not without a bit of life experience.

Luke emphasises the power of patience and hard work:

To be the first person to say something (and I hadn't heard anyone else say what John Agard said before him). If you're just writing stuff about external stuff, you don't really have such a care about it, as much as if you're writing from an inner place. It is a lot more poignant, and needs to be protected.

SPEAKING OUT ON SOCIAL MEDIA

One of the spaces that helped me in communicating and developing my mixed voice and opinions was on social media. Here I started voicing my feelings about being mixed as a way of creating space for myself and working out how I felt about being mixed. I reposted other mixed people's opinions that resonated with me, which in turn helped me validate what I felt but didn't feel ready to voice myself yet. I chatted to other mixed people from around the world too, which was both educational and reassuring. Social media can be great for developing your mixed voice and identity, although I would also be cautious about having firm boundaries around those who police your opinion (remember you don't have to respond to everyone!). I would advise that if you are sharing personal experiences to make sure they have been well processed and integrated first. I appreciate it might feel tempting to unload raw unprocessed feelings that have nowhere to go, but I would typically advise against this for your own emotional safety and to limit **trauma bonding** – a process of emotionally attaching to others who have similar unhealed traumas. Without sufficient awareness these attachments can quickly become unhealthy. My advice is take difficult stuff to therapy *first*, to integrate it, and then discuss it on socials *later*.

You can ease yourself into your own voice by following others on Biracial Lounge, MixedGirlProblems, MixedBloomRoom, Mixedracefaces and Mixedgirlmeetup, which are are all some great Instagram accounts where you can watch videos of others speaking courageously and candidly on their experiences in depth. Sophie Kanno (from Chapters 1 and 2) also runs Mixed Present – her own super-insightful space where she shares videos of herself and others: 'I use it just like it's a community. I have a series called "Shake the Room" where I elevate mixed voices.'

Affirmations for your mixed identity

Affirmations are positive statements that can be effective with repetition over time because they help rewire our brain's neuroplasticity to update the outdated and unhealthy programming we have been conditioned to practise around our mixed identity. Below are a few to get you started. When you have tried these and feel ready, you might like to try to writing some of your own:

- I embrace my diverse heritage and my unique blend of cultures.
- I am proud of my roots and multiracial complexity.
- I honour all sides of my heritage and find strength in my intersections.
- My multiracial identity fills me with pride.
- I am unapologetic about my mixed heritage.

REFLECTION

1. How have your opinions changed about being mixed over time since childhood to now?
2. What is something that you deeply wish other people could know about your mixed identity?
3. What do you feel is the hardest thing to speak out loud about being mixed?

Part 2

DISCOVER +

Chapter 5

Taking ownership of your mixed identity

CULTIVATING SELF-ASSURANCE, CLARITY + PERMISSION

#bothnothalf

Both Not Half, JASSA AHLUWALIA

Whether it's disrupting labels like 'mixed race' or complaining about being put into non-entity categories like 'other', who can blame us for having the persistent urge to just scribble all over those stupid boxes when decades of filling out hellish identity forms has taken its toll! I get a headache just looking at those institutional bureaucratic documents where you have to describe your race because no amount of tick boxes will ever be able to bulldoze or squish me or any of my cultural intricacies into line. The standard ways of micro-managing our mixed identities are *infuriating* and have rarely served our multiracial complexity efficiently. Can't I just tick all the multifarious aspects that make me very specifically me and add some more too?!!

In *People* magazine, 90s rock legend Lenny Kravitz remembers 'being forced to put all of his heritage and culture into one box – even if he didn't know how or even want to'. He told them: 'I didn't know what the hell to put, I was Native American. My great-grandmother is pure blood Cherokee Indian, and I'm African and I'm Ukrainian, and also Jewish Christian'.[1]

I think this form of frustration we so often feel is symptomatic of being born as racially non-binary people in a binary world. Gender non-binary people might identify as both male and female or neither one or something else that feels better suited to them and mixes elements of all genders. A similar system is necessary for mixed and multiracial people, who repeatedly come up against the belief that race is always a fixed and stable identity, because for us who are born in between races this concept just does not work, and I would go so far as to say it can harm us!

Laila Woozeer wrote in *The Guardian* that 'As a "mixed" person, the language to describe me isn't fit for purpose', and that we are being seen through a 'warped lens'.[2] I couldn't agree more! Without questioning and challenging how we are portrayed and represented, we are susceptible to internalising the false logic that mixed people are incessantly told about ourselves: 'You aren't whole', 'You are just a racially confused tragic mulatto', etc. Learning to cultivate an identity beyond the enforced lack thrust upon us, to explore how we might like to self-describe instead of what we are prescribed, takes courage, confidence and self-trust. 'They are increasingly confident about asserting their identities rather than simply accepting that which monoracial society assigns them. Many still struggle with the contradictions and uncertainties of navigating multiple racial identities, but there is also a growing realization that the ambiguity around biracialism is not simply our problem,' writes Remi Adekoya for persuasion.community.com after having interviewed dozens of mixed people for his insightful 2021 book *Biracial Britain*.

So, let us begin the important work of unravelling ourselves and our psyches from being perpetually caught up in that sticky and unhelpful binary projection. Along with some clarity and knowledge of our personal and societal history, we can allow ourselves to take a step back from this ridiculous rhetoric to witness it as just a projection of how a monoracial world imagines us to be, from its own perspective, rather than from ours. Freeing ourselves from the mono-misinformation is the work of untangling ourselves from the historical web of binary rules and regulations we have been conditioned to follow for decades of our life, without even realising!

HALVES, FRACTIONS + REDUCTIVE LANGUAGE DON'T SERVE OUR IDENTITY + WELL-BEING

Splitting is a psychological defence mechanism where it's difficult for someone to find the middle ground between positive and negative emotions. It's also known as binary thinking where only Black or white, all or nothing, good or bad polarities can be tolerated. When splitting is extreme it can lead to more severe psychological complications. What mixed and multiracial people are so often forced to do is split ourselves into these polar oppositional parts from the outside. Carving ourselves up with language and describing ourselves as less than whole is unhelpful for our sense of self because over time we might internalise the idea that we are not whole inside either. Yet we are still conditioned to describing ourselves in fractions and ways that we don't even like ourselves. As one Reddit user describes:

> I feel like it's mostly commonplace to use fractions (i.e. I'm (1/2, 1/4, 1/8, etc.) Asian) to describe your mix. I have always done this even though I was never a fan of it. I just felt obligated to categorize myself for others I suppose, or I was told that my fraction was kind of like this objective fact about me or added context.[3]

In the documentary *1000% Me: Growing Up Mixed*, the title itself emphasises how much multiracial children are born seeing themselves as fully whole – beyond whole in fact – as 1000% themselves!! This is in complete contrast with how so many of us have eventually come to see ourselves in adulthood – over-identified with the minus aspects, rather than the multitude of benefits from the sum of all our cultures and ethnicities. A simple way to rectify this is by consciously using a plus mindset rather than a minus one, i.e. 'I am Black AND white', which implies abundance, rather than 'I am half Black or white', which magnifies the lack.

Your descriptor! Your choice!

- How do you choose to self-identify?
- How do you feel about your current self-descriptor? (Mixed race, mixed, mixed heritage, biracial, dual-heritage or something else?)
- Has this evolved over time or has it stayed the same? Do you recall why this has happened?
- Is there a different way of describing yourself that you would like to try out?

In her poem 'Half Normal', queer Punjabi-British actor, poet and director Ramanique Ahluwalia raises profound questions about which 'half' is seen by observers as the 'normal half'? Ramanique, known for her roles in BBC's *Wreck* and Amazon's *The Devil's Hour*, fearlessly confronts monoracial vernacular and painstakingly articulates the strange myriad unspoken injustices of the mixed experience. Her trailblazing poem, with its no holds barred commentary on mixedness, will give you the chills.

Ramanique achieves something so achingly specific by fluently describing the intricacy of the *feelings in between the feelings* of being mixed and even the feelings in between those! There is a rousing boldness in this call to arms that is impossible to ignore. With lines like the following, it reads rather like a compendium of mixed emotions:

> I introduced myself once as 'half Indian, half normal. I wondered what was wrong with my brain to say something so revealing, so indicative of shame. Then I realised I'm just sharing what I've been told, trying to lay claim to a bit of that white gold, I catch myself believing the illusion that being half normal is better than being this whole beautiful fusion.

She reminds all of us of the value of emotional processing in service to our own power and autonomy, in a patriarchal, white supremacist world which more often than not shames us for it. Ramanique also echoes what Luke AG said in the last chapter, that being able to articulate this mixed experience didn't just simply appear to her overnight.

> It took a few years to write. I think it was in the summer of 2017 that I started writing it and I knew what I had on the page felt good, but I knew it wasn't finished. I had asked a question but I didn't know what the answers were yet. And then, in 2020, galvanised by the BLM movement and having had many conversations with my brother about our mixed identity... it felt like I finally knew what I wanted to say – needed to say!

THE POWER OF REMEMBERING
WHERE YOU COME FROM

How did Ramanique connect with the clarity and permission within herself to conjure up such a defiant statement to challenge the current paradigm of mixed and multiracial identity? Her defiance seems to emerge from not only knowing, but expertly *feeling* her way through her cultural roots as a way of grounding herself.

As a teen, Ramanique had a tough time navigating her mixed identity, especially with being racially bullied at school and intersectional factors on top of being mixed, like queerness, being an Indian woman and, as the darker-skinned female sibling, creating some even more nuanced hurdles.

> *I definitely started to develop a discomfort with my Indianness publicly during my middle teenage years which led to me feeling dissociated. It was a mixture of things going on at once. I was starting to figure out that I wasn't straight and, being a tomboy growing up, there was that element as well, where I wasn't the typical Indian girl, even within my family circle. When we went to India to visit family during the summer holidays, I'd be out in the gully with the local boys and my brother playing cricket – and I was very aware that none of the other girls there were doing that.*

By connecting to relatives and channelling ancestral strength, Ramanique managed to neutralise some of her adolescent discomfort involving her identity. She tells a story about her Sikh grandparents.

> *My grandparents lived next door growing up, and this one time when I was about 16/17, my grandad came over and we're all just sat around the kitchen table – me and six friends, who were mostly white. And my grandad started talking about India, including the classic story about coming over to England with only £3 in his pocket. I remember a moment where I felt really conscious of everyone around the table and what they would be thinking.*

> *It was quite a clear moment for me. My body had this reaction and my instincts went 'this could be embarrassing – what are all these people going to think about this?' And then my mind caught up and gave me the opportunity to check myself. I thought, 'No! This is an elder and you're here because they're here! You should be really fucking proud that you come from that, that's our story!'*

A voice inside Ramanique stepped to the fore and said, 'You should let him tell his story and be proud of him, because that's where you come from, and that's who you are! And whoever round the table doesn't get it, then that's on them!!' In that moment Ramanique connected with her own permission to be who she was, through her own history.

Getting a tattoo on her 18th birthday was a statement of Ramanique's burgeoning identity within.

The tattoo is an English word, but written phonetically in Gurmukhi script [Punjabi]. It's a reminder of who I am, a reclamation of my Indian herit-age, and a representation of my mixedness. As I explored in 'Half Normal', a world in which whiteness is the default can be disorienting when you're mixed. I marked my skin proudly because I knew that if I ever felt unsettled again, then my tattoo would help me find my way back.

Everything I've been navigating since then, regarding my identity, has been more of a dissection of what it means to be mixed and queer. What are my cultural anchors, beyond my family, now that my elders have passed away? How can I foster a community that celebrates being queer and brown and multiple, in a way that connects us to our heritage and lets us be centre stage?

THE COURAGE TO GET POLITICAL ABOUT MIXED HERITAGE IDENTITY

In his groundbreaking book *Both Not Half*, Ramanique's brother, British and Punjabi actor and director Jassa Ahluwalia, known for his roles in BBC's *Some Girls* and *Peaky Blinders*, demonstrates the need for a radical new perspective on mixed heritage identity. Through exploring his own journey in his eye-opening and heartfelt storytelling, Jassa describes how he was approached at the Wagah Border, the well-known border crossing point between India and Pakistan, by a man who, assuming he was a white Englishman, attempted to sell him bottled water. Jassa politely declined but the man persisted until Jassa lost his temper, letting rip in a tirade of Punjabi, much to the man's delight and fas-cination. He then summoned his friends to come and witness the 'white Punjabi'. Adopting this moniker, Jassa has created a series of comedy sketches on Instagram. Coining the desperately needed hash-tag (#bothnothalf) for mixed identity in the process then led to a TEDx Talk, and ultimately his book.

Jassa's experience of growing up in Leicester in the late 90s coincided with a UK explosion of South Asian cinema, TV and music: *East Is East, Bend It Like Beckham, Punjabi MC*, etc. I spoke to Jassa about how this cultural moment, combined with parents who thoroughly supported his mixed identity, felt magical for him, *until* society started telling him otherwise.

'I was very, very fortunate to receive the gift of that wholeness to begin with – that's something that I've consistently said was my parents' achievement,' says Jassa. His Punjabi grandfather was also a teacher at his primary school (the only brown turban-wearing teacher in the school!). So with his grandfather in a position of authority, he also felt a sense of protection and he didn't have to explain his identity.

I felt very much like my identity was fully whole and validated growing up at home. My white mum made a huge effort to make sure that both me and my sister were exposed to all aspects of our culture. Both Not Half arose from the anxiety and the feeling of 'Why can't I get back to that childhood state of joy?' The journey of the book has been getting back to that joy state through conscious effort.

At one point in his book, when he's a bit older, Jassa is joking with his South Asian friends and singing in a Punjabi accent, when his teacher reprimands him for it. Confusingly his friends are let off – and it's quite disconcerting to read, because of Jassa's innocence in the whole saga. Jassa is simply goofing about with his *own* language, that rightfully belongs to him as much as to his friends, but the South Asian teacher is clearly confused by how she should respond to his white presentation. 'Yes, that was me getting policed! It makes me think of the parallels of when bisexuality presents a threat to monosexuality for example. To understand mixed heritage, it requires you to let go of "The binary",' says Jassa.

Jassa's mum, who was a bit ahead of the curve, was understandably upset when, in early adulthood, Jassa began to express his struggles, as she had aimed to raise him in his wholeness, to support him. But at that time, the world wasn't quite set up for forward-thinking parenting. Jassa tells: 'She said, "Well, I tried to raise you so that you wouldn't have this issue. But actually you can only do so much, because, actually it's more of a society issue."' It's a really good point because unless society changes itself as well, parenting can only do so much to instil self-worth in our mixed children, and we need wider shifts to happen that go way beyond the home.

Jassa was inspired to use his mixed privilege (as a white-presenting cis male) to reform the way in which all actors are racially and culturally cast. Through his work with Equity – the trade union for the performing arts – and Spotlight, a casting platform, he has harnessed his personal experience of being mixed and white-presenting to make change. Until recently systems of recognition for those applying for roles wouldn't have permitted actors like Jassa (whose phenotype doesn't 'match' their ethnicity) to be put forward for roles different from how they appear. But with this new policy, all parts of actors' identities will be listed and made visible, (including monoracial actors with bi-cultural and bi-ethnic identities too), which transforms the process for everybody!

In his book, alongside his gratitude for getting cast at all, Jassa's sorrow at not being cast for who he really is is palpable. It's a pioneering step forward that Jassa ended up harnessing his mixed identity to instigate change beyond himself: 'My political activism was initially inspired by my longing to change how the entertainment industry thought about mixed heritage performers. My mixed heritage made me a trade unionist,' he says.

CULTIVATING PERMISSION FOR SHIFTING SELF-DESCRIPTIONS + RACIAL FLUIDITY

Like many of us, Jassa dislikes the term 'mixed race'. 'I'm not averse to people identifying as mixed race, but I personally don't want to give the concept of race or individual races any sort of positive credence,' he says. I get what Jassa means – it's what many mixed people think too as we've really had to reckon with the idea of racial categorisation in our experience.

I really want to emphasise that no matter what you have read in this book I cannot, nor do I wish to, dictate how you personally self-describe. That is entirely up to you and will be based on your particular mix and the politics of your own racial identity journey.

Remembering mixed and multiracial folk are not a racially cohesive monolith whilst also recognising the importance of these conversations is vital. All I aim to do is to invite you to keep an open and critical mind about language and think about what resonates. As Dr Root helpfully states in the *Mixed Bill of Rights*: 'I have the right not to keep the races separate within me: I have the right to identify myself differently in different situations and I have the right to create a vocabulary to communicate about being multiracial and multiethnic.'[4]

I started out back in the day as 'half-white' or 'mixed race', but now I'm 'magnificently beige', and sometimes I'm 'bombastically brown', especially if I need to support my monoracial brothers and sisters in a political sense. Today I give myself the permission to change how I describe myself racially as and when I please. There may be plenty of descriptions people have used to describe you in your life but now is the time to reconsider how you feel about it! Focus on how *YOU* choose to describe yourself. Have you allowed yourself to change this over time or do you stick rigidly to what you have been told about being mixed, by those who aren't?

Allow yourself permission to be **racially fluid** – meaning that the way you define your race is not permanent and can change over time according to how you as a mixed and multiracial person feel at different times in your life or various social situations.

Being racially fluid might look like:

- Allowing yourself to feel differently about your race at different times in your life.
- Knowing that however you define yourself it's still all 'you' at all points in your life.
- Giving yourself permission to change your mind about how you identify as many times as you please.
- Having a few different descriptors to use depending on how you feel and what situation you are in.

STANDING UP TO RACIAL GATEKEEPING TAKES GUTS

I moved to the big city of London in particular because it was multicultural compared to the closeted Surrey suburbs where I grew up, and I hoped to find more acceptance and appreciation for being mixed.

But even here I still have found myself regularly identity-policed, most recently from a white colleague when I said I was a brown woman. They 'corrected' me by saying 'well, you are only half'. To which I immediately felt instantly apologetic, then angry and stunned into silence about what on earth made them feel the need to tell me that about myself. When this sort of thing happens to us there can be a kind of self-silencing where you want to respond; you *know* and *feel* it's an injustice, but you also lack the language to self-advocate. This was a while ago, yet today I *still* feel angry that I couldn't speak up for myself in the moment and give some sassy rebuttal. Even as a therapist in her forties, I am still a work in progress! It's important to remember that as people, we are never 'finished', we are alive and evolving into our newest selves every single day, there is no finish line of perfectly resolved identity – and remember, that's all OK!

When everyone around us and in our communities appears so sure of themselves and their fixed identity, mixed folk are sometimes lacking in that understanding and appreciation of ourselves on a deep level. So often our identity has been dictated to us, rather than being allowed to naturally emerge from within. Which is why it is SO important to observe others who are being disruptively loud and proud about being mixed on their *own* terms!

Legendary entertainer and civil rights activist Eartha Kitt grew up in poverty and was abandoned by both her Black mixed mother and her white father during the 1920s and 30s in South Carolina. Known as 'yellow gal',[5] which was a term for light-skinned people, her daughter Kitt Shapiro told *The Guardian*: 'It meant someone who thought they were better than everyone else even though my mother was just a child at the time. She was horribly abused in the South.'

It is evidently clear that Eartha knew she was multiracial and always marched to the beat of her own unique drum, especially in how she described herself, even though it left her open to being misunderstood at the time. As she told *BBC Culture* before her passing:

> *They don't understand that I don't think of myself in terms of being a black person. I think of myself as being a person who belongs to everybody, but I think one should always feel this way. I think that, as long as you are feeling in terms of belonging only to one race, one nationality, one religion, that you have to be prejudiced... I am an illegitimate child, and at the same time I was not of completely black parentage. My father was supposedly a Caucasian,*

and my grandparents are Cherokee Indians. My mother was half black and all of this, and therefore my blood is of yours and of anybody's and therefore I've always thought of myself as this, and to be prejudiced against any of the other bloods is rather silly to me.[6]

I first came across the Bristol-based art collective Mixed Rage when I went to one of their nationwide exhibitions in Dalston, London. Their call to action around mixed identity addresses lack of representation, community, daily microaggressions and mixed emotions. Mixed Rage certainly don't hold back! With punk-style fanzines emblazoned with attention-grabbing slogans like 'Unapologetically Other: I deserve to be,'[7] it's thoroughly inspiring to see mixed and multiracial injustice being represented so creatively. Like Ramanique and Jassa, they bring the political messaging about mixed identity that is sometimes lacking in conversation about us to the fore with artworks and poetry, speaking up for the rights of mixed and multiracial people.

Being *instructed* by any of our communities that we are not allowed to identify as one or all of our identities is another thing that many struggle with. In turn finding inner permission to protest or to ignore them becomes an exhausting challenge. Olympic tennis champion Naomi Osaka, who is Japanese and Haitian American born, has fought more than her fair share of racial policing from both her Japanese and Black American communities (who said she wasn't Black any more when she renounced her US citizenship to play for Japan in the 2020 Olympics). An offensive headline for newspaper *The Australian* questioned: 'How Japanese is Naomi Osaka?'[8] But why on earth is it acceptable that Osaka's mixed identity is a 'free for all' to be debated by others?

Racial gatekeepers might say:

- 'You can't wear your hair like that!'
- 'You are not Black/brown – you are biracial. Stay in your lane!'
- 'Stop trying to be something you are not.'
- 'You aren't allowed to celebrate Black/brown history month because you are only half.'

How to respond to racial gatekeepers:

- 'I wonder why you feel the need to police my identity. Have you considered reflecting on your own identity?'
- 'You do not have any right to police my mixed identity.'
- 'I have every right to wear my hair like my mother/father/ancestors did/do.'
- 'I am Black/brown AND I am white. Biracial people are ALL of our heritages at once.'
- 'Please educate yourself and read the *Mixed Heritage Bill of Rights*. I have every right to celebrate ALL my heritages.'

British-Punjabi journalist Isabella Silvers isn't afraid to call out the specifically mixed and multiracial gatekeeping microaggressions. In the article 'My mixed race identity is not your punchline' for the *London Evening Standard*, she writes, 'There's a toxic online debate about being the "right" kind of mixed-race – and I hate it!'[9] Challenging the mon-oracially prejudiced narratives, she says: 'I've watched online debates dictate who can and can't call themselves Black, interviewed Miss World Japan about the backlash against her due to her Japanese-Indian background. I'm tired of mixed-race people being dismissed.'

I have also witnessed posts online declaring Bob Marley is 'not Black', because he had a white father, and even that Malcolm X is not Black because his father was mixed! It is concerning to think what this kind of pseudo 'social media authority', which too often gets regarded as stone cold fact, is doing to young impressionable Black mixed people who encounter it. Particularly for those who don't have identity-aware parents to help guide them through it. There is no 'correct' way to be mixed, just like there is no correct way for non-mixed BIPOC to exist either. However, we are often told by others, particularly those who are not mixed themselves, that there is a *right* way and a *wrong* way to be. Mixed people get told they are meant to look a certain way and have particular features, or that they are only allowed to be certain mixes, in order to be included by non-mixed people's ideas of how we should be to be acceptable. Instructing us that there are 'good biracial' and 'bad biracial' ways of being is problematic and intended to evoke shame.

Some stereotypical microaggressions aimed at policing mixed people:

- 'You are a white mum biracial': A stereotype that suggests Black mixed people with Black mums are acceptable, but white mum biracial people are not.
- 'What a tragic mulatto!': This is an old-fashioned trope, used today mostly as an online insult.
- 'Your parents must be divorced because you are mixed': An assumption that mixed people's parents never stay together because of the stereotype that interracial partnerships inevitably always fail.
- 'You are having a biracial identity crisis': Often aimed at those who don't conform to monoracial norms, with the intention to shame them for choosing to convey themselves differently from expected 'acceptable' codes of racial expression.
- 'It's just biracial tears!': A silencing tactic suggesting that mixed people don't have the right to their own mixed issues and are weaker, due to being only 'half'.

THE IMPORTANCE OF PROCESSING OUR MIXED + MULTIRACIAL GRIEF

By now you will have understood enough about why you absolutely do have the right to express grief even when family and community may not understand and try to challenge you from their own perspective. There are natural grief processes involved for all BIPOC from being racialised by society, and processing the inexplicable and unfair situations we have lived through as mixed and multiracial folk can be extremely painful and requires us to do so with plenty of self-compassion and care. The five stages of grief can be helpful – they might occur in any order.

1. **Denial:** This is where we might be in denial of what has actually happened in our mixed and multiracial experience because it's too complicated or painful, or we don't want to offend family

and community. Acknowledging what we have lost through not understanding more about our identity or having parents that didn't acknowledge our difference to them might be hard to face. Talking to a therapist, journaling or finding a creative outlet can help you to be more authentic about being mixed.

2. **Anger:** Although unpleasant to experience, anger is actually a really helpful stage of grief that can allow the injustice and sheer collective unspokeness of our mixed experience to be truly felt and acknowledged within. Simply sitting with your mixed rage and acknowledging it's there might just be enough. If you are ready to do so you can express your anger with a therapist, or by using emotional freedom technique, a neuroscientific evidence-based form of self-therapy where you tap on your own acupuncture pressure points while repeating helpful phrases and affirmations to release, work through and transform negative feelings. Doing plenty of physical exercise can also help provide a sense of relief and release.

3. **Bargaining:** You might feel helpless to do anything to change what happened in the negative parts of your mixed experience that you didn't understand at the time, especially when society doesn't acknowledge much of what we go through at all. At this stage you may be feeling like it's simply easier to just self-describe as one or the other and you may be wondering why you have to deal with such complications in your heritage at all.

4. **Depression:** This is where we really learn to sit with and lean into our sadness for any difficult parts of our mixed experience. We begin to really face what has happened in our identity journey and be still with this pain so that it can pass through us. Music is good for this stage, and stories or poetry from other mixed people can help us to move through the sadness and try to understand how others have coped with the isolation and confusion.

5. **Acceptance:** Finally, when we have allowed ourselves to reckon with all the grief stages, we start to accept the truth of our mixed challenges and we can begin to integrate our identity

with authenticity. We can now take our power back and grow and flourish, and see that although some of it has been difficult, there is also so much that is positive and beneficial about our mixed experience as well!

Creating your own mixed descriptor

We are so often told what we should call ourselves that very little time goes into imagining how we would like to describe ourselves, ourselves!

Terms for mixed people are constantly shifting and are also based on cultural context as well as how and why they are being used. Here are some current terms that mixed people sometimes use to describe themselves: **Blindian** – Black and Indian. **Hāfu** – Japanese mixed with non-Japanese. **Blasian** – Black and Asian. **Hapa** – Pacific Islander term for mixed people. Some embrace these terms, whilst others don't like them and find them derogatory. Have a think about how you feel about them personally before beginning the following task:

Create a descriptor for yourself to challenge the standardised descriptors enforced on mixed and multiracial people. This is an opportunity for you to broaden out and express the deeply held inner feelings and transmute them into something empowering for yourself when you self-describe.

You will need: A pen and notebook, magazines to cut up, scissors, glue, paper.

- Think of, or look up (in magazines), words, phrases or sentences and collage them together to symbolise your personal mixed experience.
- Intuitively and creatively focus on images and words you feel drawn towards.
- The descriptor could be anything at all that feels right to you. For example it could be one single word or a colour swatch such as 'beige' or it could be a phrase such as 'I am an optical illusion and the world cannot tell me who to be', etc. Be as artistic or abstract as you like with your wording!

REFLECTION

1. Do you feel you have permission to speak up for your identity as a mixed person? Why or why not?
2. What could help you find permission to express yourself in the way you want to?
3. Think of some courageous mixed or multiracial voices throughout history or from more recent times to reflect on that could inspire you. How can you learn from them?

Chapter 6

Our multiple realities + inherent duality

LEARNING TO UNDERSTAND + ADVOCATE FOR OUR RACIAL COMPLEXITY

> *I am history and future*
> *I am native and crown.*
> *I'm united and divided of Two Worlds*
> *unceremoniously collided.*
>
> 'HALF NORMAL', RAMANIQUE AHLUWALIA

When Donald Trump expressed distrust of Kamala Harris' Indian and Black heritage at the National Association of Black Journalists during the 2024 US presidential campaign, he implied Harris was leveraging her mixed identity in a Machiavellian attempt to mislead voters. Playing on racist tropes about mixed people, Trump said:

> *I didn't know she was Black until a number of years ago, when she happened to 'turn Black'. So I don't know, is she Indian or is she Black? I respect both, but she obviously doesn't, because she was 'Indian all the way'. And then all of a sudden, she made a turn, and she became a Black person!*[1]

In actual fact, Kamala has always been vocal about embracing *both* her Black and Tamil-Indian heritages, as is her human right to do so.

To be fair to Donald Trump, many monoracial people of all races think similarly about mixed identity, because they haven't contemplated much beyond the binary-focused monoracialism that serves them personally. It often feels like Western society is stuck in a colonial 'let's just divide and conquer everything' paradigm and hasn't quite fathomed the idea of duality yet, preferring to split things into this OR that, rather than embracing this AND that.

As Punjabi-British journalist Isabella Silvers writes for *Marie-Claire*:

It's all well and good telling the presidential candidate to 'claim Indian' instead (as one TikTok user did) but it's really not up to her. Harris has said as much herself, sharing how her mother raised her and her sister as Black within their South Asian household, knowing how they'd be seen in the world. These experiences are important, and no part of her heritage should be erased.[2]

Multiple truths about being mixed and multiracial, such as being both Black and Indian at the same time, like Kamala Harris, or Black Kenyan and white American like Barack Obama, are challenging for many non-mixed folk to comprehend, particularly in America where people are still collectively healing from slavery trauma. For decades the 'one drop rule' denoted that a single drop of 'Black blood' made you Black, however, a contentious and racially polarised political climate has called this into question in more recent times. In 2019 Kamala told *The Washington Post* that 'My point was: I am who I am. I'm good with it. You might need to figure it out, but I'm fine with it.'[3]

Miseducation and ignorance around mixed identity is also rife in Europe and the UK, where you only need to observe some of the discourse around Meghan Markle to spot that archaic views and stereotypes run riot across nations. Discussing Meghan's racial identity on *Piers Morgan Uncensored*, Black British broadcaster Trevor Philips said, 'She had to learn to be Black "on the job"', dismissing the essential nuance between Markle's Black mixed experience and his own monoracial one.[4]

The UK 2021 census shows a further 40% increase in the number of people identifying as being from 'mixed/multiple ethnic groups' since 2011 and the US now has its fastest-growing multiracial population ever.[5] People are starting to claim their mixedness now more than ever before, so surely we need some deeper philosophical reflection of how we can go beyond the dominant race binary narrative that has insisted for far too long we *cannot* be both or multiple races at once. It simply doesn't feel fair for us to continue to split ourselves into oppositional parts any more. We know all too well how human beings don't fit into neat little categories – and how binary supremacy plays out, not only towards multiracial people, but in prejudice towards trans people and non-binary people *all the time*. Yet gender non-conforming people have always been a part of Third Nations cultures, and the South Asian Hijra community – an ancient Hindu group of trans and intersex people – has existed since long before colonisation came along, just like mixed and multiracial people have too!

RADICAL RACIAL MULTIPLICITY

Let us look to pioneering psychiatrist Carl Jung, who spoke about embracing 'the tension of opposites' as one of his main concepts. Jung, who was heavily influenced by ancient Eastern and African indigenous teachings, was really onto something in his thinking approach, which recognised that the place where two opposites meet leads to a new area for psychological growth. As Jungian analysts Dennis Patrick Slattery and Lionel Corbett reiterate, 'Jung noticed that if the tension of the opposite possibilities could be held, if both sides could be heard and symbolized, there was often a third possibility, a new image that united the opposites in some previously unimaginable way, giving the client a new rush of new energy and creative possibility.'[6] What if mixed people actually had permission to explore being racially both *or all*, at the same time, rather than being told that we must split ourselves into sides. Who might we be then, given the opportunity and freedom for this new psychological expansion? Learning to speak from our duality and multiplicity with confidence, consciousness and self-awareness starts by first fully acknowledging it exists. And second by finding safe spaces where we can properly take the time necessary to unpack it and therefore see what we think and feel about it.

Stepping into our power, however, requires a safe space for a lot of internal self-reflection and thorough self-enquiry. Rooted Global Village is a space dedicated to personal and collective cultural transformation. The organisation offers courses exploring how we can challenge the racial status quo's perception of us, which we may have internalised as our own. On their website they beautifully state:

We've long thought of bi/multicultural identity – in all of the confusion it can create in us – as a bridge – an experience at the borderlands that longs for a new way to think and talk about this fragmented experience. In the crucible of these experiences we might find new ways of talking about and experiencing identity and belonging. Perhaps, too, can this ambiguous belonging lead us to explore new terrains that disturb the colonial project of race. What liberatory possibilities exist beyond it?'

That multiracial folk cause discomfort to others by existing in the 'grey area' of race doesn't mean we were 'born wrong', should stay silent or that we should split ourselves into pieces. Instead we need to learn to sit with our own discomfort, whilst also taking care in where and how we speak about ourselves so as to compassionately limit racial misunderstandings. By thoroughly honouring and delving deeper into our many sides, we can discover the true nuance of our experience and can explore both the privilege *and* the struggle of it. As we begin to get closer to learning about who we *really* are, we can start to accept our innate and racially non-binary way of being.

RECOGNISING WE HAVE BOTH PRIVILEGE AND OPPRESSION AT THE SAME TIME

We can learn to be cognisant of our privileges, such as how far we present in proximity to whiteness or being self-aware about the advantage of growing up around white people when assimilating to white codes. I do not fear the police in the way Black and darker-skinned people might do, and my light-skinned non-Black appearance has made it easier for me to navigate work environments and social spaces compared to some others. Lighter-skinned mixed people should always explore this privilege we have, as sometimes there can be blindspots that play into systemic or interpersonal racism.

Zoe Saldana, a Black mixed actor with Puerto Rican, Dominican, Lebanese and Haitian heritage, played the role of monoracial Black musician Nina Simone in the 2016 film *Nina*, for which she later expressed regret. Wearing prosthetics to change her features and taking a 'colour blind' approach understandably deeply upset the Black community. A mix of skin privilege and lack of self-awareness resulted in a grotesquely racist misrepresentation and erasure of the beloved music legend. Darker-skinned women in particular have significantly less representation in entertainment and business in comparison to those with proximity to whiteness, so consideration of this is vital if we are to be truly anti-racist and are not just leveraging mixed and lighter-skinned people to fulfil a diversity quota.

When Black British actress Francesca Amewudah-Rivers was announced as Juliette in a 2024 London theatre production of *Romeo and Juliet*, she starred in an interracial relationship opposite popular white actor Tom Holland. Subsequently Francesca was inundated with the kind of horrific racist abuse and misogynoir often aimed at darker-skinned Black women, which lighter-skinned people just don't experience. It is vital to have self-awareness of where we exist as mixed and multiracial people in relation to this.

Mixed privilege blindspots include:

- Saying 'I don't see colour' and ignoring your position in the colourism hierarchy.
- Not recognising or empathising with the specific racial trauma of darker-skinned people.
- Not recognising that darker-skinned people are highly underrepresented.
- Centring yourself in situations where darker-skinned people require space to speak.
- Not considering or doing self-exploration into whether racism plays a part in your own 'positive' self-concept.

MIXED RACE STRUGGLES ARE VALID + DESERVE SUPPORT

Just as dark-skinned experiences are constantly invalidated and unacceptably treated as non-existent, it can also easily be misconstrued that being mixed or lighter-skinned means everything is simply easy, when some challenges, like having racist parents and/or family members, are devastating and specific to being mixed race (or transracially adopted). Speaking about this candidly is not a desire to partake in 'oppression Olympics' but rather to point out the aspects that are less

THE MIXED + MULTIRACIAL GUIDE TO WELLBEING

spoken about in a society which, at this stage, only acknowledges the external impact of race.

Musician Poppy Adjudha, who is of St Lucian and English mixed heritage, spoke on the limits of how multiracial people are seen in *Mixed Messages* newsletter:

> *I don't think that as people of the diaspora we can find solidarity if we can't acknowledge the issue of otherness and the element of internalised racism and self-hatred. The idea that if you're mixed with anything then you're less of something. If you do have a mix of anything that's non-dark, then you do get a privilege and that's a real-life experience, but we have to decolonise the idea that you're lucky to have that. If we don't, I don't think there's any way to have a commonality amongst mixed people.[8]*

Having privilege AND oppression happening all at once in your experience, in a world that currently doesn't acknowledge this high level of racial complexity exists at all, is *tough*. The challenge of having to deal with these oppositional forces all at once, with nowhere to express them, brings a tumultuous psychological element. The platform Mixed in America facilitates supportive spaces for multiracial people, offering a four-week online course exploring issues like:

> *How do we balance our privilege and pain in a healthy and authentic way? How can we make sure we don't perpetuate racism, colorism, and white supremacy? And how do we make space for the very real racism, oppression and trauma that we face as mixed people?[9]*

We should acknowledge that mixed and multiracial people also suffer from plenty of regular racism – especially if they are perceived by others as Black. On top of that they may need to navigate the hurdle of experiencing prejudice from their own communities in the form of bullying and ostracisation for not fitting monoracial codes. Lighter-skinned and white-presenting mixed people are often shamed from expressing their racial suffering because it is perceived as trying to compete, or take up monoracial BIPOC space, but they just have different, unspoken, hidden and nuanced racial issues to deal with and likely don't know where to take them. So they end up having to cope with this in isolation, without community or professionals that know how to help them navigate their experience.

ANTI-RACISM *MUSTN'T* IGNORE SPECIFIC
CHALLENGES OF MIXED + MULTIRACIAL PEOPLE

It is counterproductive to anti-racism not to also be concerned for mixed people's multiracial experience. Paradoxically what we might experience are the complicated and hidden (usually internalised) effects of racism, rather than exclusively the external manifestation. Neither should usurp the other and *all* experiences must be heard. Sadly this conversation often ends up becoming competitive due to lack of safe spaces for all concerned and because of the sheer magnitude of unprocessed racial trauma from everyone harmed by racism, with a general lack of conversation about any of the nuance.

In 2021 during a heartfelt discussion in *The Face* magazine between musician FKA Twigs and Michaela Coel (the acclaimed British-Ghanaian actress, writer and director), FKA Twigs describes feeling like she was having a 'teenage crisis over being mixed race' during Black Lives Matter. 'I don't really think people are ready to have the mixed-race conversation yet, but it's coming. Maybe it's not time, there's a lot of stuff going on. I'm never trying to take up space with any of my opinions,' said FKA Twigs, acknowledging how whilst it's important to understand that light skin/mixed privilege exists, nuance and expansion is also needed. FKA Twigs goes on to say:

> I think there is a time where having a conversation about being mixed race or light skin, it does need to happen as well. I guess I feel that no one has the right to gatekeep what it is to be Black. And I feel sometimes, as a mixed-race person, [that] it can be a complicated conversation. It can be really difficult to kind of... know your place.[10]

We must also try to be mindful when overgeneralising 'mixed privilege' because there are many dark-skinned mixed and multiracial people who experience a similar lack of skin privilege to monoracial Black people. If they are only ever seen in relation to their Black proximity without others considering their multiracial need to be seen in the entirety of who they are too – this also becomes a kind of double erasure from being Black-presenting and then also being mixed. They can find themselves in danger of mistakenly being called out for being 'ashamed to be Black', like Tyla, the coloured South-African Black-presenting singer, who was pressured to give a statement to defend her apartheid-impacted multiracial identity when she was criticised for not identifying as *only* Black. In actuality, Tyla was simply trying to honour the highly politicised legacy of her own non-American multiracial background which incorporates Zulu, Irish and Mauritian-Indian heritage.

Culturally invalidating a multiracial person by telling them they are 'acting white' is also another way of undermining and isolating them from their BIPOC side. Because of course someone who has a white parent and has been brought up in a white community is going to have some whiteness about them.

WHAT IS MONORACISM?

The term 'monoracism' was coined by academics Johnston and Nadal in 2010 to describe 'a social system of psychological inequality where individuals who do not fit monoracial categories may be oppressed on systemic and interpersonal levels because of underlying assumptions and beliefs in singular, discrete racial categories'.[11]

It feels challenging to say because of how much BIPOC suffer under white supremacy, but most aren't aware of monoracial binary privilege because it *doesn't* come from skin colour but rather from not being racially non-binary in a racially binary world. If we look at the data we are starting to see mixed and multiracial people appear to be the group who struggle most with their mental health. In 2017 The American Psychiatric Association reported that 'people who identify as being two or more races (24.9%) are more likely to report any mental illness within the past year than any other race/ethnic group'.[12]

Horizontal hostility happens when groups that outsiders expect would have affinity turn against each other because of insider challenges to the community status quo. Monoracism occurs when multiracial people receive hostilities from any one of their own communities because of not fitting the racial codes. One mixed X/Twitter user was told to 'just suck it up' regarding the incessant taunting they received because 'it's reparations [for slavery]'. (The implication being they should sacrifice themselves due to being mixed with white.) This mindset, of accepting abuse and harsh treatment from your own community, is particularly prevalent in BIPOC older generations who might have internalised a helpful community 'role' as a punching bag for monoracial people who have it *worse*. The X/Twitter user presented this all as a humorous scenario. But as we learnt in Chapter 1, comedy is often a masked defence mechanism against pain that we mixed-race people use to cope.

MEDICAL DISADVANTAGES OF BEING MIXED + MULTIRACIAL

Lesser known about is how mixed people are even more disadvantaged than monoracial Black and brown people (who are also disadvantaged) when it comes to finding a match for bone marrow, stem cell and organ donor transplants. This isn't due to some genetic abnormality in mixed people (as race eugenisists like to believe), it's simply because there aren't that many people with exactly the same mix as us and so finding an exact donor match is really rare. There is always a chance that monoracial BIPOC might be a match with their parents, but as Mixedmarrow.org says: 'For mixed patients their monoracial parents and relatives will not match them and siblings only hold about a 1 in 4 chance. Finding a marrow match has been compared at times to "finding a needle in a haystack" or "winning the lottery"'.[13]

Roxanne (who you met in Chapter 2) explains how her medical diagnosis was stalled due to being both white and Black and not fitting expected racial categories for her illness:

> *Living with multiple sclerosis (MS) while being mixed heritage and queer creates a complex web of intersecting challenges. One significant issue I faced was the delay in being properly diagnosed. Initially, I was misdiagnosed with lupus, which is often associated with Black patients. At the time, MS was largely seen as a condition affecting white women.*

Roxanne had a vastly different experience when she was younger and went on hospital appointments with her mum compared to when she went on her own as a Black-presenting multiracial adult:

> *My experience exposed deep biases in the medical field, which were compounded by my identity. As a mixed heritage woman advocating for myself, I encountered systemic inequities that I hadn't been fully aware of as a child*

as when my white mother advocated for me, her privilege shielded me from some of the harsher realities. But as an adult with Black roots navigating the healthcare system, I felt the full weight of the disparities.

Roxanne further explains that her marginalised Black mixed identity adds more nuance to how 'seen' she is within disability communities as well:

Even now, Black and mixed disabled individuals are often overlooked in conversations about disability. Despite the change we drive and the voices we raise, we're frequently excluded from mainstream narratives, events and opportunities. It often feels like diversity initiatives are more about optics than real inclusion. I discovered my voice through anger. The injustice of waiting eight years for an MS diagnosis ignited something in me. I often wonder how different my life might be if I'd had earlier access to high-efficacy treatments.

Roxanne turned her anger into action:

I created a podcast to amplify the stories of disabled individuals, especially those who, like me, are often invisible in mainstream narratives. For others navigating similar intersections, I recommend finding spaces where your full self is accepted. Build networks of support, whether through community groups, therapy or close friendships. You're not alone in feeling unseen; there's power in sharing our experiences and lifting each other up!

Prejudice against mixed and multiracial people might include:

- Lack of empathy from others who disregard mixed experiences as not being valid either because of mixed privilege or because they can't relate to it and haven't sought to understand the nuance.
- Racism and monoracism from family, outsiders and community.
- Ridicule for 'acting white' when that is part of your heritage.
- Being monoracially erased from medical research and data groups.

HOW TO SUPPORT MIXED PEOPLE WHO
EXPRESS A SUPERIORITY COMPLEX

There is often hatred, shame and vitriol directed towards mixed people (especially from other mixed people) who 'unravel' their multiracial issues in public. But without discernment and grounded comprehension about *why* this could have happened in the first place, anti-racism work is stunted. Award-winning actress Thandiwe Newton (Zimbabwean and British heritage) had a very public 'mixed race meltdown'. Saying she 'wanted to apologise every day to darker-skinned actresses, to say, "I'm sorry that I'm the one chosen – my mama looks like you"' was an earnest (if clumsy) attempt to express herself about racism, in an interview with Sky News, that was not well received. Thandiwe, who appeared rather incomprehensible, was called 'cringeworthy' by many mixed people and was understandably triggering to many Black people.

As a non-Black mixed person myself, I could see that her delivery was problematic but I was also struck by how utterly desperate and alone in unpacking any of her unprocessed mixed trauma Thandiwe seemed. It was clear to me as a clinician that her unprocessed feelings seemed to spill out of her because she likely never had the safety to talk about it anywhere at all. Thandiwe and others like her who do this likely never had the community or safe space to unpack any of their identity issues and, although this is not an excuse, it does explain *why* this inevitably happens.

Certainly, expressing a sense of racial entitlement speaks to factors that require immediate addressing, e.g. the need to be validated by white supremacy. This needs to be unpacked properly with a multiracially competent therapist, but I wondered where on earth she would have gone to ask for help with this? Those like Thandiwe are often in a stranglehold of having no one to attempt to explore their challenges with, leaving them unexplored and prone to building up until the next time they become uncontainable and burst out.

Internalised racism is racism turned inwards into self-hatred felt towards the BIPOC aspect without acknowledging why there might be unresolved issues. Some mixed people who struggle with understanding their own internalised racism or privilege blindspots will express this in a way that perpetuates harm. Their behaviour should *always* be challenged, especially to prevent harm to darker-skinned people. At the same time, the further shame and rejection of mixed people who act out racial superiority can be minimised if other mixed people, in particular, actively consider how they can support them instead, rather than further perpetuating multiracial rejection and isolation. Kindly and firmly pointing out their behaviour to them, in a well-intended way, is a lot more helpful in the work of anti-racism than shunning them and doubling down on the exclusion, ridicule and lack of support they likely already feel.

How to take action
It is completely valid to have a strong negative emotional response when we witness someone acting racially superior, so honour your feelings about this. At the same time once you feel calmer you can channel the anger you feel into positive action.

What to do:

- Kindly and firmly reflect to them that what they have done is problematic and point them in the direction of helpful resources or a therapist who can explore this with them.

What not to do:

- Don't shame them or 'make an example' of them because ultimately they are suffering from isolation, low self-esteem and internalised racism. If you feel the need to excessively reprimand them as a BIPOC, explore why that might be with a therapist instead.

GETTING AUTHENTIC ABOUT OUR COLONISED + COLONISER LINEAGES

Carrying the intersection between colonised and coloniser heritage within us is not an easy psychological experience to hold within the self. It brings two or more opposing forces together inside us and can create a lot of inner turmoil, especially for those of us with heritages such as English, French, Dutch, Spanish or Belgian in our mix.

'Bi/multicultural experiences can create tension in our psyches and our bodies, unsettledness in our experience, effort in our relationships, and uncertainty about where it is that we belong in conversations about race, and in our relationship to lineages and ancestry', state Rooted Global Village. They further ask, 'What if those lineages and ancestors represented both privileged and subjugated peoples? People who enacted colonisation and those who were colonised? Where are the spaces we go to wade and play in the murky waters of those identities, and how might we explore the borderland experience it opens us up to?'

Kyley Winfield (who you met in Chapter 3) has been working through his feelings about his colonised/coloniser dynamic. 'You go back a few generations and there are affluent, officer class white people in my family. And then I assume I've got slavery on one side and people who were potentially benefiting from slavery on the other side. Thinking about that hurts my brain!!' he says. Although this was a complicated process for Kyley, learning about it also meant he could make sense of some things:

> What's really helped me is realising that Jamaicans aren't simply solely emancipated Black Africans and there's a whole mixture of people from all parts of the world there, including Native Jamaicans who I also feel a remarkable synergy with. Jamaica's motto – 'Out of Many, One People', is something I can really relate to.

Kyley has also been thinking about his name.

> My surname is Winfield – a surname that has been passed down to me. I have been trying to reclaim my surname: I was trying to have a connection with it and a therapist enquired, 'Would you change it?' And I was like, I don't know – I think this is who I am.' Then I started researching Winfield, and then found out that it has links to aristocracy, and one of the first colonisers was Winfield. There's some sort of memorial to him in the City of London. And there's lots of African Americans called 'Winfield', which I assume is because their master's name was 'Winfield', and they were his slaves. So it's like, 'Oh gosh, I've got this name Winfield, who potentially owned slaves!!'

This made Kyley think about his West Indian ancestry too: 'My West Indian relatives have a prominent European surname. They don't necessarily know about their lineage but at some point, someone probably owned my ancestors, and the surname given to them is still being used by their great-grandchildren today.

MIXED + MULTIRACIAL HERITAGE IS COMPLICATED

Clive Lewis, the British MP of mixed Grenadian and English heritage, started the podcast series *Heirs of Enslavement* with white British-American broadcast journalist Laura Trevelyan after they discovered her family had enslaved his family. Using the podcast to explore the colonised/ coloniser's horrible history backstory between both families is a courageous and helpful place to start. But looking into our white histories isn't always so clear as not all white people were colonisers and whiteness has shifted for certain groups over the course of time. You might have Irish heritage, who were subjugated by the British for example. Unravelling the complexity of our racial histories takes patience, self-compassion and mettle!

To show you how complicated it can be when getting to grips with your own 'whiteness' I will share my dad's background. Even though my dad was a proud Dutchman, he was also a Jewish Holocaust survivor who was adopted, with no known blood relatives. Jewish ancestry is complex and it dawned on me recently that I'm not even sure which kind of ethnic Jewish ancestry I actually have – whether I'm Ashkanazi (French, Eastern European, Russian and Polish), Serphardic (Spanish, Portuguese or Middle Eastern) or Mizrahi (Middle Eastern) – as I haven't felt ready to do a DNA test yet. My dad passed away in 2012, but when I think about his 'whiteness', even though he was whiter-looking than me, he didn't look 'phenotypically Dutch' – he was certainly tall, but had thick, curly black hair and features that looked more Mediterranean or Arab. Compared to my mum though, my dad's 'whiteness' still protected him on the street, in a way my mum's darker skin couldn't. When interviewed for his documentary, *Jews Don't Count*, David Baddiel's Black mixed niece Dionna said, 'I can't hide the fact that I'm Black. My dad can hide the fact that he's Jewish.'

When I was featured in a portrait exhibition of South Asian Pioneers at the British Maritime Museum in 2023, I was lucky to attend an enriching decolonial 'self-care' event for International Women's Day, held in the Queen's House, a stunning colonial building historically used by the crown and her inner circle. I glanced up at the paintings around me of the triumphant ships travelling to the Dutch East Indies in stormy seas and felt called to embrace my complicated heritage: 'I'm of mixed South-Asian Dutch-Jewish heritage and these paintings bring up a lot of complex feelings for me. I'm looking at these stormy seas and that's how it feels inside sometimes to hold this multiracial dynamic inside,' I shared when speaking at the event.

Struggles of the colonised/coloniser dynamic:

- Feeling like there is a 'war' inside you.
- Watching this conflict play out in your family system and not knowing how to explain it.
- Navigating both internalised racism and superiority complex.
- Not knowing how to be authentic about both/all of your sides.

COLOURISM + ITS SIDE EFFECTS

Colourism is probably one of the most excruciating and unspoken aspects of race identity (as we briefly touched on in Chapter 2) and we are only just starting to explore its divisive and devastating effect in the mainstream within our own communities. Also sometimes known as 'shadism', colourism was enforced during slavery as a system where darker-skinned people were historically treated worse than those of lighter skin. Closer proximity to whiteness granted 'special' privileges, e.g. darker-skinned enslaved people had to work in the cotton fields while mixed and lighter-skinned enslaved people were allowed to work inside the slave master's house. This poisonous segregation affected all who came into contact with this insidious regime based around skin tone hierarchy, and its impact has lasted through the generations. 'Brown paper bag tests' were used well into the 20th century where people darker than the paper bag wouldn't be allowed into parties and events, and the after-effects of colourism still created a lot of division within African-American communities. Today colourism exists in all communities of colour (with roots also in class-related caste system hierarchies in South Asia) and it impacts *all* BIPOC whether we recognise it or not.

As Poppy Ajudha told *Mixed Messages* newsletter:

It shows you the constructedness of colourism. We're all mixed because of trade routes, migration and colonisation and that can't be helped, but we use it as a way to elevate ourselves in these small power plays. 'I'm oppressed in this way, so I'm going to oppress you in this way' when actually we're all being oppressed by the same larger construct. It's easiest to enact that violence on those closest to you.[14]

Presenters Tan France (British-South Asian) and Audrey Indome (British-Ghanaian) hosted a powerful and insightful discussion for BBC One's *On the Cards* series where thoughtful perspectives around colourism across communities were explored, considering the different impact on everyone from dark-skinned to light-skinned people in various ethnic groups.[15] It feels like communities of colour *all* need to start having these kinds of more nuanced race conversations amongst themselves first, to then be able to segue into a more sympathetic comprehension of mixed identity.

Dr Isha Mckenzie-Mavinga is an author, poet (see Chapter 1) and pioneer of the 'Black empathic therapeutic approach'. She is of Afro-Caribbean and white Eastern European Ashkenazi Jewish heritage and has co-designed a course with Lydia Puricelli (from Chapters 1 and 4) for BAATN (the Black and Asian Therapy Network) in response to a demand from therapists of colour for 'a safe space to address the colour conundrum arising from issues around shadism/colourism and the multiracial experience'.[16]

Lydia is keen for therapists to continue to explore how skin tone hierarchies are reinforced everywhere we look:

The impact of colourism shows up through the media and in so much of the content we consume all the time, as well as society and community. That therapists are only starting to deepen our conversations around it demonstrates just how nuanced, painful and unspoken this topic is for everyone concerned.

THE ERASURE OF DARK-SKINNED
MIXED PEOPLE + THEIR STORIES

Many mixed and multiracial people are also dark-skinned and Black-presenting with entirely non-white mixes. Due to their lack of whiteness, their mixedness is often erased.

In her video *Things You Shouldn't Say to Biracial or Mixed People!* Black American and Filipino YouTuber Florence Ofelia describes the erasure she feels when people see her as only Black:

> *I love being Filipino. I love being Black. And whenever anyone invalidates my Asian side, it really hurts me. I'm very close to my mother, and I'm very proud of being Filipino. So when somebody tells me they can't even tell that I'm Filipino: Number one, Nobody asked you!! And number two, it invalidates that whole part of me!*[17]

A sense of belonging as part of a community is necessary for all human beings' mental health. Any time a mixed person has *any* part of their identity erased or is excluded from their own group(s) it's so painful, because whether you are 'too dark' or 'too light', we all want to belong, and mixed people want to celebrate all cultural sides of our heritage no matter our skin tone. What we have to take into account about dark-skinned mixed people is that there is even further erasure of their identity complexity.

Jamila Andersson, who you met earlier in Chapter 3, is a Nigerian-born psychotherapist and anti-racist activist of Nigerian and Filipino heritage. Through her story of growing up mixed in Nigeria (a former British colony) we can learn how Black-presenting mixed people might also be bullied for having 'whiter' features. Depending on the context of how and where they grow up in the world, the idea of 'mixed privilege' can sometimes be counterproductive and might work against you, even when you are Black-presenting in white majority countries. As Jamila recounts:

> *It started at nine or ten years old on my first day in primary school in Nigeria when I had just moved back from the Philippines. It continued up until I was 16. There was a lot of bullying – they said 'oyinbo', which means white person, and beat me up because of how I looked and how I spoke because I had a Filipino accent at the time. And my hair was pulled because it was*

different to everyone else's – it was always about my hair. I never wanted them to see me cry, so I learnt to just dissociate from what was happening.

Jamila shows me a picture where her hair came right down to her waist. Due to her hair not 'working' with school requirements she was reprimanded for having mixed race hair. This is a clear example of monoracism because Jamila could not help that her mixed race hair was different to other children's, and she was blamed for having this difference due to being born mixed, something that is genetic, that she cannot change.

At the time you had to braid your hair in a particular style to match with the school uniform, and my hair wouldn't hold the style because it wasn't super curly, it was a bit straight so it would just loosen up and my Filipino mother didn't know how to do my hair. The teachers would say 'oh, it's messy' and I got punished. And then I'd get beaten up by my classmates. I felt like I was constantly in a fishbowl – I just could never hide.

Jamila explains how she went into traumatic dissociation and became hyper-vigilant: 'It became the norm for my body to constantly be on high alert, thinking, "OK, What's going to happen to me now?"'

Jamila told her parents what was going on and her parents kept going to school to tell them. The punishments from the teachers finally stopped, but that turned into kids saying she had 'special treatment' for being mixed. This soon turned into jealousy over what was perceived as Jamila being 'privileged'. 'Until then I remember mixed race girl and boy twins joined our school and the attention went to the twins because they were Nigerian-American,' says Jamila. 'They had blond hair and green eyes so they looked far whiter and were bullied instead of me. That has always stuck with me because I felt guilt as now they had to go through what I went through.'

Jamila overcompensated by 'people pleasing', a trauma response many mixed people assume is a 'personality trait' where their survival depends on appeasing their community.

I found a way to make them like me. I did that by sort of emphasising my humour and laughter and wanting to do anything and everything for them. I remember my parents getting really worried because they were like, 'Why do you want so much money?' I would say, 'because I want to go to the tuck shop.' But really I was buying them things.

When Jamila made British-Nigerian friends in the UK it was the first time she felt accepted as a Black person. But then she started tanning to be darker to fit in with them. 'I became stuck in a cycle of trauma. I didn't have any friends until I came to the UK to study. So I was probably 18 when I finally started making proper friends – I had a feeling of wanting to hide all the time.' But when Jamila's skin was darker she felt like she was looking monoracial to the point she lost her connection to her Filipina Asian side, so then she started straightening her hair, not to look whiter as some might perceive, but to look more Filipina like her mother. Eventually, fed up with trying to fit in, Jamila stopped tanning and accepted her mixed race hair and her skin exactly as they were. As you can imagine, Jamila felt much happier once she finally accepted herself exactly as she was.

BEING WHITE-PRESENTING OR 'PASSING' ISN'T AS SIMPLE AS IT APPEARS

Passing originally derived from the Jim Crow era of US slavery where some people disguised themselves as white to escape the plantations. They would build a whole new life as they lived incognito as a white person, often completely abandoning their families, like the light-skinned protagonist Clare who married an unsuspecting white man in the 2021 film *Passing*. The term 'white-presenting' is more truthful to the modern experience, as people today are not trying to hide themselves, or be deceptive.

I agree with Naomi and Natalie Evans who suggest in *The Mixed Race Experience: Reflections and Revelations on Multicultural Identity* that the term 'white passing' is problematic, as it implies both whiteness as standard and deception by simply existing as you are. I appreciate shifting language isn't always easy to keep track of, but I would encourage white-presenting people who call themselves 'passing' to gently re-imagine how they feel about their true experience.

Some people, like me, might be described as 'passing' but also it's relatively obvious that I am not really white. On closer inspection my features are quite 'ethnic' looking. Whereas for others there are even fewer clues to their true heritage. It's often assumed that people who present as so much whiter have an easier time just for looking white, and in some ways they do. But also there can also be a lot of unseen pain to their experience, because of trying to reckon with *looking* white, whilst not necessarily *feeling* white inside at all. Those who 'pass' completely often struggle silently, feeling they don't have the right to claim their BIPOC aspects due to not having experienced explicit external racism. If we are taking care towards the external struggles of racism by using our privilege to protect and uplift others, we must also take care with the inner psychological world of mixed and multiracial people whose unique internal challenges are simply not a psychological privilege by any means.

Jasmin Harsono is an author and founder of the wellness brand Emerald and Tiger. She was born in London and describes herself as 'British' but 'ethnically as Iranian, Welsh, and Italian'. Jasmin has grown up being seen by most people as white because of her appearance.

> *I've always appreciated that there are some who are more 'in need' to be seen and heard, and I will always hold space and support that because we all see what happens to people of colour in the world. However, people who are mixed, like me, can be kept in a grey area and it is important that we feel seen and heard too.*

Growing up, Jasmin related more to her Iranian father and felt called to connect with her Iranian culture but she has only ever experienced being marginalised from her culture because of presenting as white.

> *I think I've grown up not feeling accepted as being mixed. On the face of it, I look like a white person walking down the street and then in a conversation someone will say, 'but where are you from? You look a bit different'. And then the conversation will eventually go down the road that I'm Middle Eastern, and in particular Iranian which is, you know, from a young age, is an ethnicity that is judged.*

Aware of her position in the world, Jasmin finds it hard to claim a right to her pain in the face of others. 'So on the outside, I've experienced an acceptance which I totally understand is a privilege', Jasmin articulates, 'because of the way I'm perceived in the world by my skin colour, but it's so nuanced because of what's inside of me and how I feel as a person and who I am.'

The death of her Iranian father, whom she was extremely close to, led to a complex feeling of disconnection from her roots.

I also lost my connection to my ethnicity because I didn't really have that identity on the outside, like other people. He was my identity, if that makes sense? On the outside and on the inside. I had my feelings where I felt strongly about who I was culturally, but it got so diluted when he died and that's probably where I spiralled a lot, where I realised that in childhood, I felt safer with him being around a little bit more so I could get seen.

But I also felt so confused because he didn't teach us the culture and language. It's all so layered – it's a feeling inside – sometimes of feeling so proud that you're from all these different countries and it's such a nice feeling to embrace. And then sometimes it feels so heavy because you're not accepted anywhere. You have to really learn to love and respect and honour yourself. That's really my life's mission!

REFLECTION

1. Consider the different ways in which you are privileged and in which ways you are oppressed.
2. How do you currently navigate any conflicting aspects of your identity?
3. What do you think you need to help you to find more clarity about your multiple and contradictory aspects?

Chapter 7

Navigating mixed trauma + mental health

HOW TO SPOT SIGNS OF MULTIRACIAL DISTRESS

Growing up mixed-race is a complicated space to navigate
My DNA is a constant public debate
Some people denigrate
Others congratulate my hybridity
To you, I'm fetishized
To others, I'm criticized
To me, I'm simply traumatized.
'MIXED FEELINGS', SOPHIE-KIM NGUYỄN

I want to share a story with you about how I came to understand more about why mixed and multiracial people might struggle to navigate getting access to the psychological support we need. In December 2022, I attended a seminar on 'Psychosis and Racial Trauma' at the Maudsley Hospital in London, where I also undertook my psychiatric placement as a clinician. A variety of diverse Black and brown groups discussed experiences in their own communities and presented information about how racial trauma might lead to psychosis due to the unaddressed psycho-social impact of racism on Black and brown mental health. These types of anti-oppressive cultural conversations in psychiatry have thankfully become more prevalent since Black Lives Matter. A vital addition of a 'cultural formulation' section to *The Diagnostic and Statistical Manual for Mental Health* (DSM-5) – used by mental health professionals worldwide to treat mental health disorders

– means psychiatrists are now more likely to interview their patients from an open-ended cultural perspective that considers racial stress. But the Western mental health system also has a shameful history of white supremacist bias in the way it has viewed Black people in particular. This dates back to 1851 when Samuel A. Cartwright introduced 'drapetomania' – the pseudo-science-based 'psychological disorder' of 'running away from your slave master' that was deemed a *mental illness*.

As the seminar progressed, I was all too aware of how little space there is for race conversations in mental health in general, but I also found myself feeling increasingly desperate to speak up on mixed and multiracial trauma, as no one in the groups had mentioned it, even though some of the presenters had said they were mixed race themselves. I felt a bit panicked by the familiar erasure of the lesser-understood multiracial identity aspect and I felt a tug of war arise inside me, of trying to be extremely careful I didn't take space from monoracial voices of colour (that I almost didn't say anything at all!) whilst becoming ever more anxious that no one was going to speak on multiraciality if I didn't. Audre Lorde's words of power, 'Your silence will not protect you,' once again rang in my head as I contemplated if this also applies to mixed people in this specific context?? I wasn't so sure to be honest!!

This was a groundbreaking seminar, and even though it physically hurt holding all this urgency inside my body, I respectfully waited until the end to speak. Finally it was my turn and the pressure inside me had built up to boiling point. It burst right open and I broke into (biracial!) tears. Nonetheless, I continued to speak through the waterfalls coming out of my eyes, telling my experiences of mixed and multiracial patients on my psychiatric placement and also honouring many mixed client experiences. I was clearly holding a lot both for them, *and for me*! All I knew at that moment was that I had spoken to many mixed people of various different cultural backgrounds during my psychiatric training who likely had never had their mixed heritage taken into account by doctors and were going under the radar. I have also had clients who have been through the mental health system, with no medical person addressing the impact of racial trauma on their symptoms.

I expressed my concern about how highly misunderstood specific multiracial challenges are, across all monoracial communities. I explained that I struggled to even know how to voice this as a clinician myself because mixed and multiracial people have never really had any spaces to talk about their specifically mixed experiences. Afterwards I still felt extremely conflicted and guilty for taking up space as a mixed person. But everyone's responses were really supportive, and a few of the mixed presenters then opened up more about their stories too. The Black men's psychosis group leader, reassuringly, came to shake my hand, and kindly acknowledged the importance in what I said, and I felt a wave of pride... and *relief*!

The difficulty I'd had in naming something so important, even as a clinician myself, taught me a lot about why mixed and multiracial people struggle to claim what actually happens to us: When and where should we speak up? When does it ever feel appropriate when there is so much non-mixed racial suffering? I was so worried about my 'privilege' that it almost became a barrier to me owning my own lived experience – such is the fear of being shamed for speaking out on mixed issues.

This is why it's so important that we become familiar with the signs of mixed and multiracial distress ourselves, which I will share in this chapter. As the statistics show, many of us are silently falling through the gaps. Health website the National Elf Service reported in 2023 that:

> *multiracial young adults [are] at higher risk of mental illness compared to their monoracial counterparts, according to US university research that cites that multiracial people had a higher prevalence of a history of the following psychiatric disorders: depressive disorders, bipolar disorders, trauma disorders, neurodevelopmental disorders, eating disorders and personality disorders.*[1]

Sophie-Kim Nguyễn is a Canadian-born social worker of Italian and Vietnamese heritage who wrote the courageous and evocative poetry in the epigraph at the start of this chapter. She is aware of how silenced multiracial distress can be:

> *Some people will gaslight because that's valid for them, because they never have had our mixed race experience – and so they can't really speak on it. And there are some mixed race people that are privileged and don't have a negative experience – that had a very positive experience. So it varies, right? We can't say that all mixed race people go through the same thing. There is diversity within the mixed race community, but definitely there can be a very negative and traumatic side to it – I feel like, when it comes to racial*

identity, a lot of families just don't want to go there. They don't want to talk about it. It's very taboo, even today.

Like so many of us she is absolutely *fed up* with having her mental health invalidated:

I've actually shared this poem with my family, and they were like, 'OK, you're doing too much,' 'You're traumatised??! That's a very STRONG word!!' And you know what?! I've just come to accept that no one will understand my experience except for myself. So, it's always gonna be misunderstood. That just comes with being mixed race! This whole entire time, I had to understand that it was not me who was confused – it's society that's confused, because I'm just not fitting so neatly in this racial category.

Many of us with 'survivor' heritages will relate to the extent Sophie-Kim is also extremely mindful of her parents' own trauma, which might explain their reluctance to engage in what she is also saying about her mixed trauma:

My dad's a refugee from Vietnam, and my mom's first generation Italian-Canadian. So they, I think, already have their own issues and their own intergenerational trauma. So when they had me, it wasn't like, 'let's sit down and talk to Sophie about this' you know, because back in the 90s (I'm a 90s baby!) I was taboo!! The fact that I was born – I was disrupting the bloodline for the Italians and for the Vietnamese – we were not supposed to mix, right? So my parents never had that talk with me.

As we discussed in Chapter 2, mixed children are often 'parentified', where we might also become co-dependent to help our parents with their survivor struggles, before our own. But as Sophie-Kim describes, when we don't focus on ourselves our mental health can be in danger:

My dad is much darker [skinned] than me and he gets misidentified racially because he doesn't fit the Vietnamese stereotype. He deals with his own challenges, having been a refugee and escaping the war, and so I sometimes feel like I have my own battle here. You know, I've tried to be a fixer, and as a firstborn daughter, I try to negate family conflict and everything. But now I've kind of stepped back, and I'm like, let me focus on myself first. Because if I can't even heal myself, how can I begin healing others?

HOW TO SPOT RACIAL TRAUMA THROUGH THE MIXED + MULTIRACIAL LENS

Racial trauma is race-based stress from racism and discrimination, like being affected by stereotypes, verbal abuse, othering or experiencing entry barriers at work, etc. This impacts *all* BIPOC, but might appear in mixed people also in highly specific ways.

Trauma responses are anxiety and fear responses resulting in panic and distress when the nervous system has been overloaded. This causes maladaptive behaviours to help someone cope with the shock of what they are experiencing. The following Four Fs are trauma responses where the brain and body starts gearing up to defend itself against perceived threat. This can show up in multiracial people alongside *other* racial trauma responses, as temporary responses that are short lived OR as patterns of repetitive behaviour that appear like personality traits.

The Four Fs through a multiracial lens:

- **Fight (Attack):** You may experience anger at racial injustices towards you because of microaggressions or mistreatment from both white and BIPOC sides. 'Mixed rage' often comes from the displacement and sadness of feeling unsafe or not being accepted in any group. This may show up as being quick to temper or aggressively rejecting others in a bid to pre-empt the rejection you have often faced.

- **Flight (Flee):** This might show up as escapism tendencies, dissociation or being prone to fantasy – where we can zone out or disappear from a world that does not accept us, into a safer one inside our head. Retreating into computer games, social media or our own vivid imagination might be a way of escaping painful realities of being mixed and multiracial that we are trying to avoid facing.

- **Fawn (Placate):** People pleasing around monoracial

individuals and groups is common in mixed people as we strive to limit danger or conflict that might arise from drawing attention to our mixedness. We may be over-eager to appease others for fear of being abandoned or desperately want to 'fit in'. We may be extremely per-fectionistic from wanting to 'get it right' to avoid humil-iation or judgement.

- **Freeze (Detach):** This might look like becoming silent or numb, or shutting down and staying away from people completely. Avoiding relationships or friendships might be an extreme way of responding to the pain of poten-tial rejection as a multiracial person. Dealing with other people might feel like 'too much to bear' and being on your own may feel more emotionally familiar and safe.

WHY IS MIXED MENTAL HEALTH OVERLOOKED?

In 2021 Samaritans UK made a statement calling for research relating to people of mixed ethnicity in response to unsettling findings from the 2012–2019 UK Census, which had shown inexplicably high suicide rates among this group, with mixed race women being the highest of all.[2] This discovery coincided with my own awakening about the lack of information and limited therapy support with regard to my own mixed mental health journey. This has often felt like shouting into the abyss, where others don't really *comprehend* how underserved the mixed community really is. All the cartoonish stereotypes about privilege and beauty are at the forefront of the stereotypical perception of us as a group but the reality is something way more topsy-turvy. In 2018 *The Financial Times* reported, 'Do mixed race people really enjoy the "best of both worlds?"' and stated that:

In the UK, which has the most consistent data set, we can see that those of us in the mixed-race group are more likely than the national average to attend a good university, but we are also more likely to be in persistent poverty and are more anxious than any other minority.[3]

Clearly this contrast between our privilege (where we are able to achieve a certain level of success) and when we might begin to come unstuck without being able to explain why, is something we should pay attention to. This combined with the Samaritans statistics seems to reflect that unacknowledged multiracial distress when left ignored and untreated might escalate.

In 2022 US celebrity polymath Cheslie Kryst devastatingly took her own life at the age of 30. Cheslie, who was of Black American and Polish mixed heritage, has a story that's been especially hard for me to ignore as a mixed clinician. Her impressive accolades included being a Miss USA winner, a lawyer with two degrees, a social justice activist and a TV presenter. The posthumous memoir *By The Time You Read This: The Space Between Cheslie's Smile and Mental Illness* describes how whilst she appeared to be living her best life on the outside, on the inside she was fighting high-functioning depression, imposter syndrome and extreme pressures to be perfect because she felt she had 'an unshakable feeling that I did not belong' and felt pressure to 'represent for all youth, women and Black people'.[4]

A multitude of combined factors should always be taken into account when examining what might contribute to someone taking their own life, but Cheslie's own words on her experiences seem to speak to an overwhelming level of responsibility and social pressure to be all things to all people. Her harrowing story does seem to reflect that whilst mixed people may feel inordinate pressure to use our privilege for good, this is often without full self-understanding of how we also face our own unique and unacknowledged challenges due to being mixed and not having anywhere to voice this. Many of the articles discussing Cheslie's mental health importantly mention she was a Black woman, but barely any of them say that she was also multiracial or how that is also relevant.

Society bombards mixed and multiracial people throughout our lives with extremely polarised projections with a distinct *lack* of middle ground; the 'positives' including, for example, 'Mixed people are more attractive' or 'Mixed people have the best of both worlds', etc., whilst at the other end of the spectrum we get 'mixed people are confused and doomed'. Without going through supported mixed development processes in childhood we might start seeing ourselves through society's polarised eyes as if it's our own lens on the world, swinging like a pendulum from one extreme caricatured version of ourselves to another. It's this lack of balance and self-clarity that may prevent us from accepting the grey area of our very human experiences clearly because we are too often performing for how others think we should be, which will eventually lead to distress and dehumanisation of our own limits. 'Positive' projections (being told we are beautiful or unique, etc.) might bolster our ego and self-image, but this can also be detrimental for our mental health when there is a lack of inner permission to properly explore the authentic challenges connected to our mixed experience as well.

Here are some of the issues mixed and multiracial people might face:

- **Co-dependency:** When relational bonds are based on a lack of personal boundaries because mixed people are so used to having our identity dictated by others, this might lead to feeling like we only exist in relation to other people's validation of us.

- **Emotional parentification:** Extreme self-reliance and self-sufficiency might stem from having to emotionally parent ourselves through our mixed identity without being able to rely on support from caregivers or relatives.

- **Racial imposter syndrome:** Feeling like you don't belong in your own racial identities might lead to perfectionism and never feeling like you belong or are good enough as you are.

- **Non-binary racial and cultural identity invalidation:** Where our non-binary cultural and racial multiplicity is completely unseen or dismissed by others.

- **Translation fatigue:** Exhaustion from trying to explain your mixed perspective to monoracial people so that they understand you.

- **Self-erasure:** A tendency towards invalidating or ignoring our own mixed experiences can lead to feeling a lack of identity.

- **Internalised monoracism:** Internalised messages of hatred specifically towards the multiracial aspect of ourselves.

- **Internalised racism:** Internalised messages of hatred specifically towards the BIPOC aspect of ourselves.

- **Internalised prejudice:** Internalised messages of hatred specifically towards the white aspect of ourselves.

Dr Mish Seabrook, a psychotherapist and resilience coach of British Indo-Trinidadian and Irish heritage, has worked with many mixed clients on their self-development journey. I wanted to know what she thinks about the mental health pressures we experience of feeling we constantly need to prove our 'cultural credentials' and receiving so much identity invalidation (which has been proven to significantly affect mental health in general, particularly for non-binary people).

Dr Mish: It puts you in a position of questioning your OWN existence. For example, 'As a person, SHOULD I even exist?' It gets really fundamentally existential and such interrogations can be quite fracturing to our psyche I think. I'm not sure of many people who have to contemplate whether or not they should exist, as a person, as a being. So I think it's a real existential wound; should I even exist? In this person's eyes, am I allowed to exist? Because they want me to justify my actual existence. That's how I see it as a therapist. You'd ask 'what are you?' to an alien. You might say, 'What's that? I need to identify what species it is?' It's the 'IT' that comes with the 'what?' Your very existence is being chronically questioned. Unfortunately it doesn't always come from a benign place – I've experienced a lot of aggression behind this question.

Namalee: I agree and it's usually us looking at ourselves through the eyes of others isn't it? Rarely through our own lens. Where do we get a chance to develop that with all the external pressures of who we are meant to be?

Dr Mish: Yes, it's 'Am I allowed, in this person's eyes, to EXIST?' 'AM I allowed to exist – because they want me to constantly justify my existence?' Constant questions of 'What are you...? Having worked with mixed clients who sought me out because they know I will 'get it', speaks to me when I'm faced with it [the uniqueness of the mixed and multiracial experience], as a mixed person, and as a therapist. So when they come in and go 'this thing happened' or 'this person said this' or 'am I even alright to exist in this world?' I get it!

Dr Mish breaks down the negative impact that the constant racial interrogation can have:

It's kind of like, 'I don't understand 'IT' and 'I need to understand how to categorise 'IT'. It's your very existence that is being questioned, which is a very dangerous thing if it happens over and over again.

Namalee: For me, being interrogated about my race is compounded by intergenerational trauma where my grandparents were literally not allowed to exist any more because of being Jewish. You can see how my example might relate to others in how different aspects of their own cultural intersectional identities can overlap and be emphasised to the point it all gets too much to cope with.

Dr Mish: Yes – because mixed people are CONSTANTLY forced to question their existence – whether they 'should be here', where they belong, etc. That might make you think about NOT being here. Over the years of being asked 'what are you?' I still get that look where people stare right into my face. So I experienced the question in a look sometimes, they don't even have to ask it, but I know it's there. They know it's there. It can feel like a fracturing of my existence.

Namalee: That is very relatable. How do you feel about the Samaritans' statistic about mixed women taking their own lives more than other groups?

Dr Mish: I'm heartbroken by that. You weather your own storm – but to hear those statistics makes me go 'Oh, shit'. This is a universal truth for many women. And we're not riding it out very well. So something is going drastically wrong. There's something being missed or not spoken about or not acknowledged, or all of those things. Because we know about a lot of people in society, we love to think that it's a more 'tolerant' society, but I'm not entirely sure I believe that.

Multiple factors affect mixed and multiracial mental health

Overlapping intersectional racial and cultural factors can affect a mixed person's mental health. This will include:

- **Phenotype**: how do you present racially? e.g. Black-presenting.
- **Ethnicity**: what is your ethnicity? e.g. 'Caribbean and white English'.
- **Culture**: what is your personal culture? e.g. 'An English surfer in the UK'.

The above presenting factors will then meet the combined factors of:

- Age and generation.
- Nationality/national status.
- Neurodivergence (ADHD, autism, dyslexia, dyspraxia, etc.).
- LGBTQIA+ (queer, trans, non-binary, intersex, etc.).
- Class, education and poverty factors.
- Disability and health issues.
- Adverse childhood experiences (ACEs).
- Trauma.
- Environment.
- Religion and/or spirituality.

MENTAL HEALTH REPERCUSSIONS OF OVEREMPHASISING APPEARANCE

The concerning mental health statistics have made me think about my own experiences as a mixed woman and how since very young, like many women of colour, I was also sexualised, with heavy focus attributed to my 'mixed beauty'. It made me wonder about the link between this unhealthy and obsessive fixation on our external appearance from others and the internal impact on mixed mental health. *All* women regardless of race have an intolerable amount of pressure placed on how we look, but when it comes to being mixed, this seems to happen to an excessive degree.

I was scouted by model agents as a teenager and I feel grateful that I did not sign with anyone, knowing that even with my proximity to whiteness, I would never have fitted the beauty standards of the time enough for it not to be a risk. These days the modelling industry is somewhat healthier, with many more diverse models who are also activists, which was unheard of when I was growing up in the blank canvas 'look good and shut up' late 90s era. The increased pressure from the modern stereotypes of mixed beauty standards seem to double down on us with a crushing force, which author Remi Adekoya also acknowledges in his concern for 'the central role of looks' in mixed women's 'self perceptions and identity trajectories', in *Biracial Britain*.[5]

One of the most outspoken and photographed stars of the last decade is the Black mixed Ghanaian and English model/activist, Adjoa Aboah. Known for her distinctive red cropped hair, freckles and gold capped teeth, Adjoa founded the brilliant platform Gurlstalk and has consciously used it to speak out about her own struggles. In doing so she has helped amplify many other voices about all kinds of mental health issues. Talking to Krishnan Guru-Murthy for Channel 4 News in 2019, Adjoa told of an attempt to take her own life and how a culmination of factors led to her depression and addiction.

'I wasn't Black enough and I wasn't white enough,' Adjoa said about being bullied for being 'Black and posh' which didn't make sense to her boarding school peers.[6] 'Being mixed race was confusing – we were posh, but we weren't white and we weren't black enough either,' she says of herself and her sister. 'A lot of Black kids at my school were international so they had all grown up in Nigeria, Ghana, etc. and we come from London, brought up by a white mother. Lots of things [were] going on in my head.' Adjoa self-describes as Black, which makes her feel 'solid' and 'part of a community'. Part of her motivation for founding Gurlstalk was to create her own community because in her own words: 'that's all I ever wanted growing up'.

UNBELONGING, ISOLATION AND HYPER-REJECTION

Adam Nimoy, son of Leonard Nimoy who played the iconic 'half-human half-Vulcan' Dr Spock in the original 1966 cult sci-fi drama *Star Trek*, recently tweeted a heart-warming story of how a young girl once wrote to Spock (the character) about the prejudice she faced for being biracial. His father replied in character, saying: 'Not everyone will like me. But there will be those who accept me for just what I am,'[7] I was incredibly moved by this when I saw Adam's post, imagining this poor girl feeling so desperately alone that she wrote a letter to a fictional character for therapeutic support. Spock's advice was *fantastic*, and many mixed people commented on his 'biracial icon' status in the comments section. I do wonder about all the other mixed and multiracial people who have never had anyone to talk to about the overwhelming loneliness of this experience – one that is magnified when you grow up in a non-multi-cultural area with no one to reflect back at you that what you are going through is a completely normal multiracial experience.

Nina Camara is a Black mixed activist of Guinean and Slovakian heritage and a community leader. As founder of Reunion events – a social media platform exploring cultural and lifestyle themes related to mixedness – she hosts groups and seminars to support and widen discussions around mixed identity. Nina has some valuable advice about integrating your mixed identity, based on her own experience as someone who had to become an expert at this with a lack of resources, due to growing up in a town where she experienced plenty of 'other-ing'. Nina explains that 'Some were curious and others would think there was something strange about you.' In Slovakia, Nina had limited access to Black culture, particularly African-American pop culture. She grew up in the 90s, just after the fall of the Iron Curtain when the introduction of democracy and open borders was just starting and access to Western culture was still opening up. So as a result, she's become adept at finding her own methods to navigate being isolated from your culture. 'Try to educate yourself,' advises Nina:

There's still not a lot for us to consume in popular culture. So try and find stories from people with a similar background of being a mixed person and properly look around for it. Aim to do what the mainstream culture is not doing. It shows us a very limited and stereotypical picture, so you have to deep dive to find the real 'image' that is totally different most of the time to what we are being served [as mixed people]. And make sure to focus on the positive things as well, not just the challenges!

Whilst Nina encourages all mixed people to seek community, she recommends to also be prepared for what might unexpectedly emerge for you emotionally in mixed spaces, once you actually have the chance to speak about what you have been through with others for the first time.

What I have noticed in mixed communities is it can be very easy to get negative, because there's a lot of things that weren't discussed [in our childhoods] – that should be discussed. And people are coming back to this after years of not speaking about it. So only do what is comfortable for you.

I appreciate Nina's sage-like awareness about this because it's very easy to overlook self-care and overdose on trauma in mixed groups as there are so many people all with their stories to tell, which is brilliant of course, but having it all happening at once can be *a lot* to absorb. Never be afraid to excuse yourself or take a break if you need it. Mixed people often struggle to navigate boundaries too so maybe consider it an opportunity to practise yours!

Nina is aware that trauma is a popular subject on social media, but once again she encourages a steady, slow-paced approach to your mixed self-care.

You don't always have to deal with the most complex dramatic thing just because it's a popular conversation! If, like me, you grew up in a small town and knew of few Black references, don't suddenly put pressure on yourself. You don't need to know everything about Black American culture, for example, if you didn't grow up like that. Look for what's relevant to you and build from there.

REFLECTION

1. Have you ever suffered from mental health issues? Did you consider how the mixed part of your identity may be impacting things?
2. Can you think of any scenarios where you see yourself relating to any of the signs or trauma responses listed in this chapter?
3. Have you ever considered going to therapy to speak about your mixed race or multiracial identity?

Chapter 8

Finding the therapist for your mixed identity

TIPS FOR CHOOSING SOMEONE TO SUPPORT YOUR MIXEDNESS

I wasn't birthed to
make any
sense to a
system
designed to /divide/
and /conquer/ me,
from the
Inside

'+TRICKSTER+', NAMALEE BOLLE

The mainstream therapy industry has only relatively recently started to properly reckon with and awaken to the effect of race, intersectionality, marginalisation, oppression and trauma, and how this all affects our mental health. Mixed and multiracial people are still the minority within the minority when it comes to race, so finding a therapist to help you navigate things can be very helpful. Therapy doesn't always suit everyone, so pay attention to what feels right for you personally. If you decide to go the therapy route, then it's really important to think about exactly what you are looking for from your therapist so that you can make the most of it and really get what you need from it.

Take the time to deeply consider what your goals are and get clear about how you actually want to benefit from therapy. Your therapist is there to support you on your journey but it also helps to be aware of what you need from them too. I will share a story about a previous therapist I worked with who was great with some aspects of my identity, but we only skimmed the tip of the iceberg when it came to my mixedness. One time I showed them a drawing I made of a fluorescent multicoloured alien flying through outer space with broad and open wings. 'Tell me about this?' they asked, clearly intrigued. 'I think this must be my soul,' I said.

'It seems to have a kind of longing for something, Namalee, in its expression... What does your soul long for I wonder?' I considered the question for a bit and then spoke intuitively, 'It longs to be known, truly witnessed and allowed to... well... exist.'

My therapist's response started promisingly. 'There seems to be a sense of deep longing within your experience,' they noted, but then came a myriad of distracting observations about how I might be longing for various things.

'Yes, you are right,' I robotically and rather performatively obliged. Had my therapist been more curious and less directive, it would have provided the space for my own embryonic mixed voice to emerge. I left the session agreeing with my therapist's perception of my drawing as my own, rather than discovering my own narrative about my own drawing. Looking back I can see that the alien I drew was simply longing for other aliens. Giving me some space to consider how I felt a bit more might have allowed me to link the alien with my literal racial alienation, and longing for my own community! My therapist unknowingly played directly into a common mixed and multiracial narrative of me accepting what I am told about my identity from any external voice but my own. This isn't bad, because re-enactments of past experiences happen in therapy to help us to *finally* recognise reoccurring issues, but if the therapist is not multiracially aware they won't know this often happens in our mixed experience, and I didn't recognise it either, so it was missed...

CULTURAL HUMILITY + ATTUNEMENT IS ESSENTIAL FOR MIXED PEOPLE

Cultural humility is being extremely curious and open-minded about cultural and racial experiences without inflicting a stereotypical viewpoint or bias. This is important for all BIPOC and especially so for mixed clients who often don't understand how the multiracial aspect of their experiences might have impacted them, and they need a little help in unearthing it. Someone who uses plenty of enquiry and invitations to find out more about your own personal unique experience will be beneficial, as there will naturally be things they don't know about the mixed experience too if they aren't mixed themselves. I have had therapy with various monoracial therapists and some of the issues I have had with them (although they all had different benefits and talents!) is that they still all shared some preconceived, generalised views about what mixed people experience.

Some therapists of colour will also have monoracial blindness around mixed clients too. I cannot emphasise enough how a good therapist can come from *any* racial or *any* cultural background. What's important is that they have anti-racist and anti-oppressive understanding, so that as a client you won't have to spend time teaching them about intersectionality or explaining other distressing things to help them understand you. Mixed people need to be seen in their true narrative to heal the racial attachment trauma from parents/caregivers and society, so encountering a monoracial therapist who works to make us feel truly seen and heard, who is willing to go beyond what they think, to deeply listen and be open to experiences that differ from theirs, is a very soothing experience for us!

What sometimes happens for mixed and multiracial folk is that we may have large gaps in our identity development process (as we learnt in Chapter 2) that we need to revisit and rediscover to get in touch with our authenticity. Who we really are may be hidden behind layers of performing under binary monoraciality. Or there might be some pain points we perceive as 'depression' but on deeper inspection are actually unspoken anger and grief that we have dissociated from or struggled to explain because we have never allowed ourselves permission to feel our true feelings in case they are unacceptable to one of our communities.

We might be lacking some 'inner ground' of our identity stability or we may have just ignored huge swathes of our culture due to shame from simply not having access to it. Regardless of your specific experiences in the world, or whether you relate to anything discussed so far or not, if you haven't had a safe space to explore, express and discover how you really feel about being mixed, it's hard to know what you really think about your own experience and how things might have affected you, whether positively or negatively.

Mixed + multiracial impacted emotions might show up as:

- **Dissociation:** Feeling ungrounded in our own mixed identity experience may lead to disconnecting from our body to stop feeling altogether, as a way of self-preserving and checking out of our true emotional experience. This may present as compartmentalisation of our experiences and psychological 'splitting'.

- **Toxic positivity:** Over-identifying with the positive aspects and projections of mixed stereotypes (beautiful, unique, rare, etc.) and ignoring any negative emotions that require processing to keep up appearances and stay away from mixed pain.

- **Guilt:** Having more skin privilege than monoracial BIPOC can make us feel guilty for what they go through, especially with our parents. It is important to distinguish that whilst we do have privilege, mixed privilege is not the same as having 'white privilege'.

- **Shame:** You might show a lack of self-value through self-deprecation, etc. Maybe you feel embarrassed or ashamed when you are around monoracial people and you might reduce your visibility with a slouchy posture or hiding in some way or by staying quiet.

- **Depression:** Feeling isolated and alone without a group or safe spaces with people who understand that your mixed experience might make you sad and teary for extended periods. Maybe you have been bullied or ridiculed and are constantly pushing this down.

- **Resentment and/or rage:** This might be towards parents, society or other people who invalidate or misunderstand your mixed experience. We might even turn anger towards ourselves in a kind of self-hatred.

CHOOSING A THERAPY STYLE

There are so many methods to choose from and it's really up to you to find the style that fits your personality and your needs. This might mean some trial and error as you work out what is right for you. Some styles you might want to consider looking at are person-centred, narrative, existential, or internal family systems therapy as these can be helpful approaches to working with mixed identity. Internal family systems therapists, for example, incorporate 'parts work', which can be helpful because of our tendency to split ourselves up. Some therapists like myself use an 'integrative' approach where we use a mixture of modalities together, rather than a strictly purist approach, which I personally find is a natural fit with being mixed, but it's entirely up to you to choose what feels right. Look for therapists who flag up they are an 'anti-oppressive, anti-racist and trauma informed' practitioner. (There are some links for where you can find therapists in Chapter 12.)

CONSIDERING YOUR INTERSECTIONALITY

Consider if maybe a potential therapist's various intersectional identities might be useful in their lens for understanding your experience: Are you looking for Black? Brown? LGBTQIA+? Cisgender? Disabled? Neurodivergent? Roma? Traveller? Refugee? Immigrant? Muslim/Jewish/Christian/Hindu, etc.?

Don't ignore these aspects of your identity, as they sit together with your mixedness. It's unlikely that if you have multiple marginalised intersecting aspects you will find someone who ticks *every* box, but at least one box will be helpful in making you feel understood without having to over-explain your identity to the therapist. Ultimately if the rapport is there between you both and the main intersectional aspects are covered, or even if they aren't but the therapist has an anti-oppressive approach – that is a promising start. If you are neurodivergent, in particular if you are autistic or ADHD, you might have a preference for a particular style of therapy as well, so be mindful of this when deciding.

WORKING WITH AN LGBTQIA+
INTERSECTIONALITY-FOCUSED THERAPIST

Addam is a queer, Indian and white psychotherapist from Bristol, who wanted to find a multiracial therapist of colour after having therapy with a few different white therapists himself. Not only did Addam struggle to find a mixed therapist in his area, he also knew it would be near impossible to find someone who was mixed South Asian.

> *Even the very term mixed, for a lot of people, doesn't incorporate Indian. The Black and white stereotype is usually what people think of. It's particularly my experience within the gay world as well, where people expect you to be Black and white. But yet, there are so many of us from various different cultural backgrounds that are mixed.*

Eventually Addam found a therapist that fitted the bill in a few ways that were very helpful: 'It turns out, there was ONE other queer male mixed therapist in Bristol, from a Black background. So we are very different, but it was great to have that connection on quite a lot of levels.' Addam's therapist noticed something very important for people from mixed intersectional backgrounds – that the combination of his gay trauma of learning to overcompensate was resulting in excessive care-taking and putting other people's needs before his own. This showed up in therapy when Addam was habitually trying to put his therapist's feelings *before* his own, which also spoke to 'mixed race people pleasing'. This was exacerbated and even more apparent because his therapist was Black mixed, and Addam is white-presenting Asian mixed. Addam's therapist helpfully called him out on this, 'Not in a harsh way, but he flagged up to me that I needed to stop prefacing everything with the idea [that I'm privileged],' explains Addam. The therapist then made an important invitation when he said: 'I really recognise that our experiences are different, but it's OK to be you.' As a result, Addam says, 'I think that it took me a while, in a way, to just be open.'

Addam felt a lot safer with this therapist than his previous one:

> *It was very, very different from, for example, with a white therapist before, where I opened up on a traumatic experience I had at university, when I was tone policed by a peer in class, in front of everyone... And then I had to explain what tone policing was to my therapist.*

So on top of Addam's own distress, he also had to educate his therapist, which was exhausting for him.

I don't have an expectation, obviously, that every therapist must know every single term under the sun. But actually, when you're processing something in relation to identity, it's nice to be in the process, and not to have to pause from it, to explain, because there's so much burden put on minoritised folks to experience this! But then we have to teach people about it too... I just want to be in therapy in the same way that everyone else is!

INNER CHILD WORK

Alex Lewis, a psychotherapist (who you met in earlier chapters) is conscious to focus on the 'child self' that often gets 'parentified' for so many mixed race folk (as we learnt in Chapter 2). From his own experience both as a client and therapist, he advises:

It's important for anybody to ask themselves, what were their experiences growing up as a mixed race child? How do you think it impacted you? What can you remember?

There's a lot to be said about just giving your 'child self' the voice that you needed back then. Growing up myself as a Black person and as a mixed person, I just sort of felt shut down and not OK and I just kept everything inside myself. I realised actually, there were a lot of things I wanted to say that I didn't. So what I do when working with a mixed race client is to look to help to give that younger self a voice. There's a lot of stuff that we can revisit like that and it gets hidden because we switch it off inside.

He is also mindful of how much we have usually taken on for our parents:

If our parents can't contain our fears and our experiences then we just have to sit in them and hold it all ourselves. A therapist will hold that for you, and then feed it back to you in a way where you feel understood. As a child. The fact that our parents can't and still find it difficult to hold what it means to be mixed is hard. Imagine how much that weighs on a child, and what sort of impact that may have on their mental state?

ADVANTAGES OF WORKING WITH A
MIXED + MULTIRACIAL THERAPIST

Having sat in as the mixed client and in the mixed therapist's chair Dr Mish is able to bring her own experience of both sides to working with mixed clients. 'Just like I sought someone out, people have also sought me out, because they also want to have someone opposite them that absolutely gets it,' says Dr Mish.

As a client, Dr Mish, who is of Indo-Trinidadian and Irish heritage, specifically sought out a mixed therapist for herself and explains how it allowed her to let go in a way she didn't feel she could with previous therapists:

> I'm not saying there's no value to sitting across from someone who's not mixed. But in this particular area of intersection for me, it felt like relief – like I could finally relax. As I was telling her about my story, there was just this 'knowing' she had. She KNEW and there's something around having that essential part of your identity so delicately held.

Dr Mish explains how the therapist self-disclosing her own mix was reassuring and the difference of working with a therapist who can create a sense of ease in the relational bond vs someone who is trying hard to prove they are 'culturally competent':

> It wasn't a superficial 'getting it'. It was just 'I get it'. There's a sense of peacefulness, of being totally seen: her understanding of the pain and the loneliness of this specific experience. And the shame that gets associated with it, that frustration. I didn't have to 'choose any side'. There was no assumption of needing to choose. It was just 'you're here and I see who you are. And I understand your experience.' And it's like, 'ahh I can take a breath. That's what it feels like to exhale.'

For people who might be considering going to therapy but might be unsure, Dr Mish advises them to do some self-enquiry first:

> If they sit in the 'Oh, I don't really think about being mixed' camp, then they might need to think about going to therapy! It's an opportunity to look at everything that being mixed brings. Including the good times and all the challenging times as well. Because someone may have normalised

the aggression that is behind the questions, or the fascination with your skin or your hair or your shape or your features. Also to be able to explore your privilege and the oppression as well – to get into those really opposing places and to own where that is in you. And to do the exploration of both is – it's vital.

Dr Mish says it's important to consider that:

You may have normalised a lot that's not normal – that these things are scrutinised and held in such fascination or curiosity or disgust. So I'd say for any mixed person who's ever experienced any of that to go and sit with some-one who will 'get it' because it will absolutely lighten the load. It just helps you go 'hang on, that's not OK is it?' And that can be a joyful and painful experience. And to just be sat with you and to put everything together is really the best gift you can give yourself. Because it's who you are. It will shape everything that you do and every interaction.

MIXED MEN + THERAPY

Alex is conscious that as a cisgender Black-presenting mixed race male therapist, he hasn't seen many others like him in his practice, although he has worked with plenty of mixed female and monoracial Black clients. He is empathetic of the challenges for Black mixed identity as a male that they might be reluctant to explore in therapy:

This is my personal opinion based on my own experience in therapy, not necessarily clients' experience. Going to therapy brings up a lot for people of all ethnicities around identity and challenges who they are. My identity has been a delicate topic for me to address, as we are raised to believe through unconscious programming that the world is either Black OR white, and you can be this and only this and mixed raced men are literally the 'in between' so to unpick this thing which we have worked so hard to forge throughout our life can be a scary process. And that may explain why men of mixed ethnicity stay away from therapy as they're scared about what it might unearth for them.

Alex encourages mixed men to be courageous in service to their mental health, but he admits it's a challenge:

For myself, to go from being othered for being mixed race (particularly the Black side of me) to then coming to a place of self-love when you have internalised so much racism, is a difficult proposition. And then equally there is another part of us – the white side which we must come to accept as well. The difficulty I had was that I embraced my Blackness so much that I removed my white self from the equation, so then I had to go through a journey of accepting my white side, which for me represented oppression and hatred.

Being racialised as a Black male brings up having to uphold stereotypes of masculinity, which might be why they might not go to therapy. 'I guess all it boils down to identity for me and how there is a reluctance to question that in therapy because as mixed raced men it's been a challenging topic,' says Alex. 'My Blackness became a protection as well, so shedding that defence and exploring my identity can leave me extremely vulnerable.'

Alex is hopeful for men however: 'The fear about facing identity is sad, really, if you think about it, because it's there for all to see – so why would you not face it? But I understand that maybe facing it is difficult, because there's something that's been pushed down throughout their lives,' he says.

Mixed men might struggle with:

- Letting their guard down.
- Being negatively stereotyped for their looks, e.g. 'player', 'pretty boy', 'scary', 'aggressive', etc.
- Knowing when they need or can ask for support, having been socialised as male and therefore someone who shouldn't show emotion.
- Being honest and authentic about how their experiences have impacted them.

WORKING WITH A MONORACIAL THERAPIST

It is not always easy to find a mixed therapist as there are still not many of us out there (although I'm finding more all the time), and as with all therapists of colour, just because a therapist is mixed that doesn't guarantee that they have done the anti-racist self-enquiry necessary on themselves!

Through the Black and Asian Therapist Network (BAATN) I joined their Mosaic group – a process group for therapists who are of either mixed or bi-cultural backgrounds. This helped me to see that monoracial therapists with bi-cultural backgrounds are particularly likely to understand and empathise with the mixed experience due to the cultural crossover in their own identity, so look out for them, whether Black, brown or white! The key is knowing what your needs are and being selective about that. Don't be afraid to leave if something feels unsafe, but also try to be discerning that you are also trying to challenge yourself, so long as you are not being harmed. What feels intolerable might just be you expanding your emotional tolerance and capacity to handle difficult feelings.

Helpful questions to ask when interviewing a potential therapist:

- Have you worked with mixed and multiracial clients before?
- What do you think is important when working with mixed heritage?
- What transcultural/anti-racist/intersectional training have you done?
- Which therapy approach do you use and could you tell me about it?
- Are you a member of BAATN, or your own country's equivalent?
- Do you consider yourself an anti-oppressive anti-racist practitioner?
- Are you trauma informed and/or trauma trained?

Most therapists offer an initial meeting which is either free or at a discounted price. Don't be afraid to be discerning when looking for the right fit for you. Be bold!

REFLECTION

1. What are you looking to explore in therapy with regard to being mixed?
2. What is your budget or how much are you willing to pay?
3. Would you prefer online/remote or face to face?

Part 3

THRIVE +

Chapter 9

Building community + connection we deserve

SEEKING SOLIDARITY WITH OTHERS + CULTIVATING SUPPORT TOGETHER

I hope you find the home that you have always wanted.
I hope it's walls are sturdy, built on the ground that you had to
dig through way too early.
I hope you find the love that you are craving, both from yourself
and from others.
I hope you find acceptance in the places you got tired of looking.
'MULTICOLORED HEART', INDIRA MIDHA

One of the biggest barriers we have to truly understanding ourselves with depth is that we lack a mixed and multiracial community where we can reflect and bounce our experiences back and forth. I often wonder how many other types of marginalised groups would have developed their identities to such a high degree without the support of like-minded folk whom they met in groups where they could safely share and develop their ideas together. For instance, would LGBTQIA+ movements have become so influential had they not first got together and spoken to one another about their common experiences? Having a sounding board is vital to build the confidence and comradeship that mixed and multiracial folk rarely get the opportunity to develop on their own terms. Part of what prevents this happening in the way it does with other groups is the general lack of permission we have internalised from monoracial society's ideas about us.

I first heard about the 'Mixed Girl Meetup' when it popped up on my Instagram feed in early 2020. Rather tellingly, as someone who has started a few communities myself, it had not occurred to me yet that mixed people could actually get together as a group... that it was even *allowed*! Yet it was exactly what I have craved my whole life, without ever realising.

'So I just put it on this website, meetup.com, and thought if one person shows up, great!', says Shakayra Stern, the Jamaican and Austrian born, Switzerland-based events organiser, author and founder of the Mixed Girl Meetup, about organising her very first event. What happened instead was remarkable!

That moment, I will never forget, it really changed my life. I researched various Black owned establishments and settled on a local restaurant bar in Harlem. When I arrived, there were ten people at the table waiting!! There was an older lady who was around 58 or older, she was Puerto Rican and Black. And she said, 'I really wanted this my whole life and I never knew it could exist – you brought it to life.'

Shakayra was so moved by the vulnerability of the stories that were shared.

Another girl was saying she wasn't even going to come because she was so nervous. But she said, 'I called my fiance saying I was going to turn back and he said, 'If you don't go – you're gonna regret it forever.' Even now it makes me feel super-emotional because I just started this because I felt super-lonely. And all of a sudden, it's bringing all these people together who are just like me and it's gonna sound silly but I love Marvel comics – it felt like this inner kind of superpower to put such a meaningful event together.

Shakayra wasn't always so confident about building her *mixed empire*. After telling an ex about her unbearable loneliness, he suggested she start the group to meet mixed folk like her. Shakayra was reluctant at first: 'I kept filling out this form online, to start my group. And every time I started, I stopped, because I kept feeling like "WHO on earth would get this?!!" "Would anyone even be interested in this?!!"' The critical voices got louder. 'This is egotistical – I don't know why I am doing this?!'

As I stepped down the wooden stairs into the cosy West London eatery to go to my first Mixed Girl Meetup, trepidation crept into my thoughts, and although I am usually pretty outgoing, I recognised I, like Shakayra, was feeling especially vulnerable about this. But the greetings from a bubbly sea of excitable beige and brown faces put me immediately at ease. I scanned the room again. There were a few people who looked like they could have been from my family, more than the people in my *actual* family! Overwhelmed, I was inspired by the totally unexpected sense of comfort and familiarity.

Shakayra expertly went round the table asking everyone to introduce themselves. I was awestruck, listening intently to everyone sharing their mixes and personal stories. I realised I had never in my life been anywhere with this many mixed people in one room, let alone all sat around a table eating and drinking together. Our sole purpose of being there was an invitation to discuss the experience of being mixed!! It felt utterly *magical*!

FINDING ACCEPTANCE AMONGST YOUR MIXED + MULTIRACIAL COMMUNITY

By reaching out into the unknown and taking a risk, Shakayra was met with many like-minded people who were all looking for the same community she was. Sometimes we can get so stuck in our feelings and used to feeling isolated that we cannot imagine it ever being different. But I love how Shakayra used her feelings to take action and mobilise herself into power by creating what she always needed, and therefore she ended up providing the space she craved for others too. The 'permanent outsider status' of being mixed *became* the driving force to reach out for the deeper connection she dreamed of.

Shakayra remembers there was huge relief and deep healing when she finally completed her first Mixed Girl Meetup:

Of course I'm in host mode and I want everybody to feel comfortable but as much as I help others heal, I also heal myself in the process of holding it. There is a huge warm, fuzzy feeling I have every time I've done an event where you just feel so seen and understood. To be present, especially in the times that we're living in now, is so special and really rare. At these events no one looks at their phone, because we are so immersed in conversation and we feel that we can just let go and really be ourselves.

She goes on to describe how the group is a chance to *let go* of the mixed mask we often wear:

> *It's a feeling of belonging, warmth and understanding. There is no script that I'm following – I'm always in the moment. That's how I want the people that come to events to be as well, because I think a lot of us go through our lives, having to be people that we're not sometimes. It's like there's this facade to fit in and always be adapting and hey, we do it really well – but inside there's a longing for 'I want to let go of the show' and 'I want to speak about my experiences'. I don't want to feel like I'm having to prove myself.*

Shakayra is conscious of how creating our own community can support our mixed mental health in ways we may not recognise we need.

> *Being mixed is a lot of proving yourself about things that are actually quite normal [for others] – proving yourself to your family, proving yourself to teachers, friends, or partners – and it's always this 'not enough' feeling that crystallises in us. Others have community that accepts them immediately, but because we don't have that, there's this 'proving yourself' that can go really far, with people even showing photos of their family to strangers, just to prove their existence, which is really painful.*

THE MIXED + MULTIRACIAL EXPERIENCE IS A GLOBAL HAPPENING

As well as London and New York, Mixed Girl Meetup has been held in Los Angeles, Milan, Paris and Amsterdam. 'We also have a following in Austria, and in many cities in Germany and Switzerland!' Shakayra says about the overwhelming response to taking Mixed Girl Meetup global which resulted from to going online during Covid, when she built up a following from some unexpected places.

> *I could actually reach continents like Australia and Asia. So we had people from Japan and Australia join us. I have brought speakers in too – for example there's this influencer that is pretty big on Instagram at the moment. She's Australian and African American and she came in talking about the*

mixed experience in Australia. So that's also something that in Europe, we wouldn't know about. Finding out she went through similar experiences despite being in Australia felt like a big comfort as we all realised we are not going through these things alone!

Learning about the breadth and depth of global mixed experiences is key to Mixed Girl Meetup.

We have had people also in African countries like Ghana, Nigeria and South Africa where we have a big following – and just hearing the stories and the similarities to me is still baffling. Because I always thought I was alone. And this is what's so powerful – actually we're not – we cross borders! But when you're sitting in your bedroom as a child and you think like, no one's gonna 'get it' – you feel so weird and misunderstood. And then you go out in the world and hey, there's actually people that get it!!

Shakayra is keen to reiterate that the purpose of community is not to isolate ourselves from other groups for being mixed but, as Shakayra puts it, 'more so to find a sense of belonging, build our confidence and heal. By getting to know ourselves better and feeling more confident, we can get back out there, feeling energised and reconnect with other groups to share our authentic selves with the world!'

BUILDING YOUR OWN MIXED + MULTIRACIAL CREATIVE COLLECTIVE

Pauline Jérémie (who you met in Chapter 2) founded *Middleground* in 2019 – a beautiful online magazine incorporating artwork, short stories and poetry where mixed and multiracial people can express themselves. Building *Middleground* has helped Pauline overcome some family issues too.

I had been sitting on that idea for maybe a year, or year and a half. At the time I was facing a lot of racism within my own family and I felt very isolated in that situation and I just needed to find community to normalise it, talk about it and work through it I guess, which I couldn't do with my family or with my friends who weren't like me. And so I sat on that idea for a little bit.

Similarly to Shakayra's reticence to start Mixed Girl Meetup, Pauline also wasn't sure if anyone would respond to her desire for a magazine collective:

> For a while I thought I was the only one who experienced something like this... I couldn't find a community to join. I was in Edinburgh at the time and I just kind of decided that maybe I could build that community instead. But because I thought I was the only one experiencing it I thought 'no one is going to be needing this'. And there was part of me that thought it would just be a project for me and I just didn't see the point in doing that.

Pauline decided to put the feelers out to gauge interest for something more communally mixed.

> So instead, I started looking for other mixed people – writers especially or people in the arts, all around the UK. And I reached out to them and I asked them if something like this existed – a magazine specifically for and by mixed people where we collate our lived experiences and are given a place to talk about it – would that be of interest to anyone? Do you think this is something that would be valuable for the community at large? And everyone said, 'YES!!'

Like so many other mixed people I have spoken to, Pauline cares deeply about being of service to the mixed collective and wants to include many voices, rather than just her own. 'That way it felt less self-centred – something that actually could benefit other people. So then I built it!' She remembers:

> I met our first poetry editor at the time, who was doing a master's in poetry, and we ended up working together! And that's kind of how Middleground was born. The idea was, we would put out two issues a year and publish between about 13 and 16 artists and writers. In each issue, solely mixed race people from anywhere in the world [can speak] on whatever mix and whatever topic they want to talk about. But it had to be on something about mixedness. I have a background in creative writing so that's why it felt very comfortable for me. I know how powerful the arts can be, how powerful creative writing and visual arts are in telling your story. That's why I chose that medium. And the rest is history!!

LEARNING FROM INSPIRATIONAL ROLE MODELS AND MULTIRACIAL REPRESENTATION

'I really wanted to focus on people who were putting things out into the world – authors, presenters, musicians, politicians – you know, people who had that public presence and I explore what they have to say,' announces British-Punjabi journalist Isabella Silvers about *Mixed Messages*, her award-winning Substack. The weekly *Mixed Messages* newsletter is bursting with interviews and essential info about mixed identity and the platform also hosts its very own event, *Mixed Messages Live!* (You have met Isabella already in Chapter 5, as she often utilises her confident mixed voice to advocate for much-needed mixed representation in the media.)

'Three and a half years and nearly 300 guests later – I'm still here!!' Isabella smiles proudly. And so she should. *Mixed Messages* has interviewed a staggering number of mixed thought leaders including Leanne Pinnock, Hanako Footman, Jordan Stephens, Elizabeth Yu and Ben Bailey-Smith. We *really* have been crying out for this level of mixed representation, for, well, our entire mixed lives! She says:

> The whole point of Mixed Messages is to show that there's not one way to be mixed, because I think that was something that was irritating me when I saw girls on Love Island say that their type was 'mixed race guys'. And I'm like, Well, I 'know' what you mean – but I don't know if they knew 'what' they were saying. What they meant was someone who had light skin, you know, Eurocentric enough features to be 'palatable'.

This fetishisation magnified how much the conversation also excluded Isabella from her own group. 'It was just irritating me!! Also I don't feel white and also don't feel Indian for various reasons – so I felt like 'am I not mixed race too? Because they are using it only as a shorthand for Black and white men??' So, I was like – I want to be here, and take my space. I want to be in this [conversation]!' she asserts.

Mixed Messages newsletter is also an insightful and educational platform for everybody, including Isabella herself, who is constantly reflective of being in a process of understanding more about others' mixedness. 'I've learned something from every single person that I've spoken to,' she says. 'It's been really unexpected. I didn't anticipate that I'd learn so much, but I'm glad.'

Over time Isabella's perception has shifted and she has become increasingly self-aware in how she makes enquiries with interviewees about their mixed heritage.

When I started, I was looking for answers to fit my preconceptions. I remember I was interviewing someone, and I always ask everyone you know, 'What's your background?' 'How do you identify?' And when they had basically not said, 'my mum is Black and my dad is white', or whatever, I noticed myself, keep going on at them – 'but what's your mix?' And I realised. They don't owe me that, and if they don't want to identify as 'half and quarters' or 'my mum was this, and my dad was that' – they don't have to tell me that!

This moment of checking in on herself and recognising that mixed identifying comes in many variations was clarifying for Isabella.

I really noticed like, 'Oh, I'm really trying to get people to give me what I expect... But actually, shouldn't I be open to the whole question: "How do you identify?" Shouldn't I be open to the way that they identify?' I think I thought that everyone would think the same as me. And I think I thought everyone would have this confusing 'identity crisis' or issue and actually, some people are very comfortable and have been very fine with it over time, and it's not been a big issue for them.

Through *Mixed Messages* Isabella has discovered how important it is to grant those she speaks to their own autonomy over their identity. 'You know, some people don't identify as mixed, they [might] identify as [just] Black, etc.', continues Isabella.

With one interviewee, I asked her to do the newsletter and she said, 'I'm happy to do it. But just so you know I just want you to know that I identify as Black – is that fine?' And again, I open myself up to go, 'Yes, that is fine!' And that's what I'm trying to portray. And now I say to everyone that I'm open to them disagreeing with me and challenging me. It's nice to expand what I think, because that's the whole point of what I said I was trying to set out to do!

STARTING A MIXED + MULTIRACIAL PODCAST

Militantly Mixed is a podcast about race and identity from the Mixed-race perspective created by US-born Sharmane Fury (she/they/Sir – aka daBlasian Blerd). Sharmane purposefully capitalises the word 'Mixed' which I totally applaud! Sharmane is multigenerationally Mixed and comes from a US military family on both sides. Growing up she was surrounded by many Mixed people, and when she left home she felt the need to reconnect with the Mixed community.

> *At the time I started the show, there were no active Mixed podcasts. There were a few that had made it to six or 12 episodes, but then just dropped off. So for at least a year before I launched Militantly Mixed, there wasn't anything and I wanted to find community. I grew up VERY Mixed, my parents are both biracial, so all my uncles and aunts and cousins are Mixed.*

'I have grown as a person so much since starting the show,' says Sharmane about her personal journey of starting the podcast.

> *You know I joke about how creating it was selfishly motivated – but really I was seeking community because I felt starved of it. I wanted to be able to have conversations where I wouldn't have to pause and offer context every other sentence and it took finding other Mixed folks to have that. Even if people don't share your Mix, they may share your experiences of otherness, and a bond is created in that.*

Sharmane says about feeling outspoken compared to others in her generation:

> *I think it is so hard to find and connect because from my generation (Xennial) and earlier, we were taught to not discuss such things as it could make people uncomfortable. For me, I was frustrated by why I had to be the uncomfortable one, having to deal with people othering me but me not being allowed to be vocal about my Mix and my multicultural heritage. I think a lot of people have struggled with that too.*

As the show began to grow, Sharmane not only found an audience but met people she was hitting it off with and made plenty of real-life friends.

I was noticing that exposure to other Mixed folks' experiences was teaching me a lot or clarifying something I was thinking or feeling and didn't have a way to name yet. As those things were becoming obvious to me, I started to change ideas, behaviours, etc. If you were to listen to the show chronologically now, you can hear my development over time. It is a strange but beautiful and unique position that I am in, having access to listen to me grow as a person. I think learning new terms or ways to express my feelings about my Mixedness or Mixedness in general has been such a gift!

'Be your Mixed ass self' is the rather epic Militantly Mixed podcast slogan (which is also available on t-shirts and hoodies!).

The concept of 'Be your Mixed ass self' which became the motto of the show was something I actually yelled at a guest on episode 11, because she was feeling so much doubt about her claim to Mixedness, because of her appearance. It was because I was having these conversations that the idea just bubbled up inside me and burst out like a geyser because one thing I cannot abide is a person not feeling they have access to claim themselves. Regardless of presentation or access to culture because many of us have families that assimilated to whatever the dominant culture of the countries we ended up in. So over time I realised the work of the show and me was to help guide people into finding the confidence to be their 'Mixed ass selves'.

I have received countless emails and DMs that were grateful for the show because they had not heard or, in some cases, met other Mixed people. And Militantly Mixed was helping them not feel so alone. I would cry from some of the messages I would get because this strange little thing I did by pressing record on conversations with Mixed people was turning into therapy for so many people, including myself!

To anyone thinking of starting a mixed podcast, Sharmane's advice is to 'start from your comfort zone'.

I love talking to people about being Mixed and their various cultures. I cared less for the 'issues' that faced us necessarily and more about the personal stories. I think that is why the show was so successful. It's because people could hear my genuine interest in the subject and as a member of the community myself there was authenticity in the work.

There is so much room in the podcasting game that WHATEVER aspect of Mixedness you are more comfortable and confident in or most curious about needs to be the angle you start from, and if other times other things come up, it can be incorporated but you don't have to kitchen sink your Mixed podcast at the start. Start from where you are most passionate, confident and comfortable and build from there. We need more Mixed voices, we are not in competition with each other. There is so much room for us in podcasting!!

Start your own mixed community

Now that you have heard from those who did it themselves, there is nothing stopping you from building your own mixed community. Maybe you can gather a group of mixed friends or maybe you prefer to go solo; you could simply start a WhatsApp group or Slack to put the word out and build it from there!

You might consider:

- What kind of topics would you cover?
- Are there any themes you would focus on – e.g. art, fashion, mental health, etc.?
- Would it be online or in real life?
- How could you promote yourselves on social media?

REFLECTION

1. Have you ever joined or considered joining a mixed race group? If so, what was your experience?
2. What you would like to say in a mixed community space? What would you like to share about yourself with like-minded others?
3. What is something you would particularly like to experience from joining a mixed group?
4. What are your fears about joining or starting a mixed community?

Chapter 10

Acknowledging + harnessing your mixed superpowers

HONOURING YOUR UNIQUE QUALITIES + MULTIFACETED WAYS OF BEING

*If you are in need of a hero to improve your social skills, relationships
or business profitability
Then fire the multiracial bat signal into the sky!*
'DO YOU HAVE SUPERPOWER PROBLEMS?', KYLEY WINFIELD

Many mixed people I have met are aware (on some level) that having to
rise up through the monoracial projections; archaic stereotypes; desperate need for community; deficiency of authentic deep conversations
about being multiracial; lack of proper mental health support; and a
total absence of understanding about our specific perspective can be
a challenge to say the least!! In many cases I would say these hurdles
have also meant we develop some extraordinary superpowers, talents
and useful adaptations. And no, I'm not claiming mixed people are
some kind of *super race* – I'm certainly not talking about eugenics here!
I'm simply talking about the gifts and talents mixed and multiracial
people develop *despite* everything that's put in our way. Like borderless
flowers we bloom through random edges of the pavement, up through
the cracks in cement like it's the perfect home. Mixed and multiracial
people have always thrived, strangely and sublimely, between the borderlands of race and culture. And we shall always continue to flourish,
sometimes in slightly alternative ways!

Right now you might be reading this with mixed emotions, wondering if it's really OK to feel thrilled about being mixed? You might find yourself fretting over whether we are even allowed to use the term 'superpower' to describe our attributes. That's exactly my issue! If society gives us the message that we shouldn't openly celebrate ourselves then I want to reiterate that mixed people celebrating themselves *isn't* at the expense of anyone else whatsoever. Mixed and multiracial people are phenomenal exactly because of the multiplicity within us and the unseen resilience and adaptations we have made, often due to our very specific and individual (depending on our mix) lens on the world. A lens born from being distinctly at the margins and intersections, with a very particular vantage and interesting viewpoint.

YOU ARE ALLOWED TO CELEBRATE YOUR MIXED AND MULTIRACIALITY

'"We now feel proud to be mixed": The blessings and biases of being biracial' reads a headline from a 2024 *Guardian* interview with *The Half of It* authors and *Mixed Up* podcasters, Emma Slade Edmondson (British, Jamaican and white) and Nicole Orcan (American, Ghanaian and Filipino), who have pushed the mixed conversation into new territory with their bold, honest mixed storytelling.[1] When I first read this headline, I remember thinking, 'Wow! I've never ever seen that statement said out loud before!' I felt so much pride arise within me when I saw it. But there's grief too, in realising it's taken so long for us to get here... Stating our mixedness proudly and defiantly doesn't mean we think we are better than anyone else. I want to remind you again that it is OK to celebrate yourself for being multiracial – just like it's OK to celebrate yourself for being from any other marginalised group!

I remember feeling like I was doing something clandestine simply for retweeting a post promoting Irish Mixed Race Day. Yes. you read that correctly, Ireland have their very own Mixed Race Day! As do Brazil (*Dia do Mestico*), and there is also a 'Hapa' day as part of Asian-American Pacific Islander Heritage month. Los Angeles even has a mixed race festival called Free to Be Fest (founded by Dr Jenn Noble) – how fantastic is that!! And did you know about the patron saint for mixed race people? St Martin de Porres was born in 1579 in Peru to a Spanish nobleman father and freed slave heritage Third Nations and African mother.

St Martin looked after the sick, founded a residence for orphans, and represents barbers, innkeepers, public health workers, animals and those who seek *racial harmony*! The contributions mixed and multiracial people have made towards society are enormous, breath-taking and astonishing. Yet – if I ask you to tell me off the top of your head who some of them are you may struggle, because historically mixed legacy has been largely ignored, lost, hidden, forgotten and mono-washed (did I just invent a new word there?!).

Of course we cannot, nor would we ever wish to, deny the huge importance and significance of *all* of someone's sides, or indeed, how anyone wishes to racially identify. I also appreciate that identity definitions and what being mixed and multiracial means has also shifted over the course of time. But, today can't we please *also* acknowledge stories pertaining to celebrating people's multiracial identity *as well*, so that we can learn about how others have managed this mixed terrain before us and be *inspired* by them?

I've yet to be convinced being mixed hasn't impacted the work of the mixed race people listed below in some way or another. But rarely, if ever, in my life have I seen any in-depth explorations of how the multiracial and bi-cultural aspect impacted a prolific person's work. As a multiracial person and therapist I *know* this aspect deeply impacts our lives, whether we choose to see it or not, and I know I'm not the only one who would love to see more representation of this aspect of our historical identity in literature, storytelling and cinema.

A list of a few prolific mixed people who you may or may not know are mixed:

- **Bob Marley:** Reggae legend (Jamaican and English).
- **Sade:** Songwriter and style icon (Nigerian and English).
- **Merle Oberon:** First mixed Asian actress to win an Oscar (Sri Lankan, Maori and British).
- **Charles J. Pedersen:** Pioneering and Nobel Prize-winning organic chemist (Japanese and Norwegian)
- **Frida Kahlo:** Pioneering feminist painter (Indigenous Mexican, Spanish, German and Hungarian-Jewish).
- **Gigi Hadid:** Model and presenter (Palestinian and Dutch)
- **Eddie Van Halen:** Rock legend (Indonesian and Dutch).

- **Stromae:** Musician and DJ (Belgian and Rwandan).
- **Charles Mingus:** Jazz pioneer (African American, German, Chinese, Third Nations).
- **Mel B:** Spice Girl and author (Jamaican and English).
- **Rudd Gullit:** Footballing star and activist (Surinamese and Dutch).
- **Central Cee:** British rapper (Guyanese, Chinese and English)
- **RAYE:** Record breaking music artist (Ghanaian, Swiss and English).
- **Akala:** Author, activist and rapper (Jamaican and Scottish).
- **Shakira:** Singer/songwriter known as 'The queen of Latin music' (Lebanese and Colombian)
- **Lewis Hamilton MBE:** Formula One racing champion (Grenadian and English).
- **Dame Tracey Emin:** British artist (Turkish Cypriot, Romany and English).
- **Adriana Lima:** 2010s supermodel (African, Portuguese, Indigenous Brazilian, Japanese, Swiss and West Indian).
- **Yasmeen Ghauri:** 90s supermodel (Pakistani and German).
- **Pam Grier:** Blaxploitation actor and feminist icon (Black, Hispanic, Chinese, Filipino and Cheyenne).
- **Zendaya:** Actor and fashion icon (African American, Nigerian, German, Scottish).
- **Kehlani:** Singer, songwriter and dancer (African American, Native American, Caucasian, Spanish, Mexican and Filipino)

So, we've talked a lot in this book about the challenges, but what are some of the aforementioned positive qualities that mixed and multi-racial people might develop that can help us to shine in life?

THINKING OUTSIDE THE BOX

This literally comes from living *outside* the concept of a race tick box. We often end up comfortable in free fall with NO BOX AT ALL. Growing up having to tick 'other' because there wasn't a box for me anyway eventually meant I got to a point where I kind of didn't care any more about fitting into racial categories. I was done – in a good way! Wanting to belong doesn't automatically mean we want to be trapped inside a box either!

If you don't agree with what I'm saying though, no problem! I appreciate that if anyone puts mixed people in a box, especially other mixed people, we will jump out faster than a Jack in the Box! In fact, for all who disagree with what I'm saying, I fully support you in your independent thought, but I hope you also consider it might be... because mixed people don't want to be boxed! ... Just saying!

To those who stick rigidly to their *boxed in boxiness* you 'really just don't know what freedom feels like, maaaaan!' (said in Lynn from *Girlfriends* voice). And as a result of thinking like this, others might decide we are weird, maverick, odd, defiant, rebellious, bizarre, unique, etc. But this is really because mixed people are sometimes like those folks who are still alive at the end of the apocalypse; we survive the racial and cultural 'monoscape' over and over, with no acknowledgement that this is how we are living. So we might be a bit bent out of shape, a bit different, living somewhere between our trauma responses and a totally radical new way of envisioning things – making the most of it all!

Punk icon Poly Styrene was the Somalian and Scottish lead singer of the band X-Ray Spex, with a legacy for being an outside-the-box thinker. In the 1970s she screamed operatically from the top of her lungs: 'Identity is the crisis can't you see... When you look in the mirror, do you see yourself? Do you see yourself on the TV screen? Do you see yourself in the magazine? When you see yourself does it make you scream?' like some kind of shamanic mixed prophet grieving our past, whilst summoning in our mixed future![2] In *I Am a Cliche*, the documentary about her life, Poly talked about how being mixed race made her feel like an outsider growing up and that's why she joined the punk scene. But even there she was *still* unboxable compared to other punks. Speaking to *Dazed* magazine, her daughter Celeste said: 'My mother was always going to be an outsider in anything she did. Even when she joined the Hare Krishnas, she was always on the edge of it. She was too unique to ever fit in.'[3] Flexibility and open-mindedness are both terms associated with outside-the-box thinking. We might not all be punks like Poly, but if you have a desire to kick out old outdated ideas with a confident authority, you might be more of a mixed punk rebel than you think.

Clara is an art teacher of Zimbabwean and Irish heritage:

I've never really fitted into a box, specifically, especially for me as I had no other mixed heritage peers and there was no one in my area that was of mixed heritage! So I think having that experience growing up has maybe made me quite mindful of being a little bit outside, metaphorically and physically, of not really fitting in.

I feel it hasn't hindered my viewpoint – my viewpoint has always been very open, especially having parents that were not of the same race being together and married, which was again, very different from my peers when I reflect back on it. So I think I'm good at this because I don't attach myself to an identity as such, I feel like I'm more of a chameleon! I'm not sure if that's a good way to express it, but as someone that can kind of adapt, and doesn't feel the need to stay within a box, but feels like I can go 'in and out' because my experience has been that I can adapt into various different situations and different groups. I'm really good at shapeshifting!

BRINGING INNOVATIVE + PROGRESSIVE PERSPECTIVES TO HELP TRANSFORM THE WORLD

In his TEDx Talk 'Poetry, Diversity and The Camera Lens Conundrum', Luke AG (who you met in Chapters 4 and 5) discusses his work being on the other side of the lens as a Black mixed advertising strategy director. Luke queried the white, classist gaze within the agency he works at, using his mixed privilege to facilitate change: 'I was like, "We are casting so many Black, brown and mixed people. And there's no one [like us] on the other side of the camera...!!" I found it so strange!'[4] he says. Luke pointed out not having BIPOC people behind the camera lens was not conducive to the bigger picture.

I also thought that it leads to really BAD storytelling, because you're forcing something into another story, which is not great. You can tell when some-one's doing something they are not comfortable with. So I created this kind of 'initiative' to change the diversity of that agency. We had like 13% Black, Asian and mixed race creators out of like 36 of us. And our US office is now like 55% – so it's been really successful.

'We opened an office in Stoke-on-Trent', Luke continues, 'And that's not a racial thing, necessarily. It's because we were telling a lot of working class stories for advertising and everyone went to film in Durham [a working class English Northern city]'. But the people behind the lens were from Cambridge or Oxford, he says, acknowledging the class disparity. 'I was like, if you want "diversity" and to tell working class stories, you need working class people behind the lens as well!!!' Luke utilised his specific multiple lens on the world, in service to considering all marginalised groups and overlapping intersectionality. This is a bit like what Jassa (from Chapter 5) is doing in the acting industry:

> It's like all of these struggles are aligned – the solidarity struggle for trans and queer liberation ideas of nationhood and a borderless future. And class, and social inequality in class, and even very fixed ideas of the separation between spiritual traditions ALL need challenging, and they're all aligned!!

Jassa reminds us that we all lose out when we shun radical multiplicity, and how working across intersectionality struggles strengthens all of us at once, no matter what group(s) we belong to.

> The world in which a trans person feels that they're at home; that they belong, is also the same world which makes people feel very much at ease in who they are. The hierarchical, separating binary mindsets that underpin all those old ways of thinking all come from the same place.

> That was probably one of the biggest discoveries for me, along the way. It was like, yeah, that shift from thinking just about me and MY particular problem, and then realising that, oh no, actually, it's all coming from the same place! And, if we tackle the core, then everything else sort of falls into place. That has to be a political struggle, because we're sort of reshaping – it's like a reappraisal about how we structure society. That can't just be done through a, you know, 'biannual diversity panel'!

As 'racially non-binary' people, mixed and multiracial folk have plenty in common with non-binary, bisexual and trans people, who also share multiplicity and duality in their experience too. This alliance feels intrinsic and obvious, although race is something separate to gender identity. Nonetheless all of these groups are marginalised in some ways that cross over and all of our identities are so often policed for being non-binary.

COMFORTABILITY WITH MULTIPLICITY IN MANY FORMS

Challenging as it may be in the beginning, holding multiple truths or perspectives within us (as we explored in Chapter 6) is something that mixed people might develop pretty well in various areas. I have learnt to apply this non-binary approach with conflicted emotions – giving myself permission to hold all supposedly oppositional feelings inside me at once. The glorious spectrum of human emotions doesn't appear neatly in tidy, boxed sections either, although in my opinion the mental health system doesn't particularly acknowledge human *emotional* complexity either (but that's a story for another day!).

I remember when writing one of my therapy training essays we were asked to explain our reasons for working in the way that we did. I trained as an integrative therapist, which means I incorporate various modalities together (psychodynamic, humanistic, existential and transpersonal) and I wrote how I would *never* be able to be a 'purist therapist' because mixing together styles is in my natural way of thinking and being as a multiracial and multicultural person. Nothing else actually makes sense to the way my mind works and I have always naturally embraced mixing things together! When I worked as a stylist I purposefully clashed colours and mismatched things on purpose. It was all done with the intention of trying to get the fashion industry to imagine a world that felt more culturally accepting of colour and that wasn't all 'matchy matchy'. I'm not racially or culturally matchy matchy so why should my clothes be?!

Similarly, when conducting and analysing her research for her doctorate, Dr Mish was questioned on whether the combination of what she wanted to do was possible. Dr Mish challenged the binary perspective: 'Being mixed really helped me when I was writing my thesis because people were telling me that I can't use "this and that" way of analysing "because they don't work together"'. Dr Mish says, 'I was like I KNOW they work because "I work" as a mixed individual and it works INSIDE my being.'

UNDERESTIMATED STRENGTH + RESILIENCE

There is a stereotype that enforces the idea of mixed people being 'weaker' due to being 'racially diluted'. But balancing the coloniser with the colonised inside us, I would argue, might cause lesser traversed monoracial mortals to self-implode. Don't *ever* underestimate yourself as a mixed and multiracial person because being both or more races takes *immense* grit and stamina!

In the research paper 'Viewing multiracial people as resilient rather than burdened', it was reported that:

> *Social and Psychology Personality Compass find reason to believe that multiracial people, though often the target of bias directed at those of a single racial minority, might possess notable and unusual powers of resilience: the ability to switch between racial identities to adapt to circumstances; and 'reduced essentializing of race', meaning, those who are multiracial might naturally feel less defined by race than others do.*[5]

This was captured in a video for UK news platform *Novara Media*, when Black mixed journalist Moya Lotharian-Mclean interviews an elderly white woman who proceeds to tell her Enoch Powell (the UK politician who gave the infamous anti-immigration 'rivers of blood' speech) 'had the right idea'. The woman then confronts Moya about 'not being from this country' all whilst smiling at her. 'It's nothing personal' the woman tells Moya.[6] It's a marvel that she's able to keep her focus in the face of such unabashed racism and a testament to Moya's Black mixed resilience. Mirroring the disarming aura of politeness, Moya does not lose her cool, her boundaries, her backpack or her sense of humour. 'What would you say about someone like me, who's mixed?' Moya asks quizzically, and then ends by comedically quipping about how she's 'off "back home" to Shropshire'.

As we have seen throughout this book, mixed people can demonstrate an utterly phenomenal level of resilience and self-sufficiency in the face of a whole range of very specific types of adversity. I believe this is because of developing capacity from having to work things out on our own from early on in life, and by this I mean often without much attachment support around being mixed. Resilience coach Dr Mish points out: 'I do think mixed people have an incredible resilience that we don't even really acknowledge we have.' She explains how being made to deal with constant interrogation meant she took things into her own hands with a reframing approach. 'In a way for me it's all about taking all the staring and the "fascination" and going "well I must be truly amazing then! For everyone to be THAT bothered about me!"'

At times when she's felt challenged, Dr Mish has a word with herself: 'I tell myself I'm a physical embodiment of being able to hold what someone else would class as opposing forces in me. That is powerful, you know, like when superheroes hold that ball of power! That's what I picture, a ball of electricity of power and force!' she says. The workplace is a lesser discussed area where mixed people might have struggled especially with diversity training, which doesn't always consider the anguish of mixed people's experience of being made to choose sides. This was something Dr Mish experienced too:

> They put all the white people together and all the Black people together. It was a big workgroup and the trainer said 'go to your group' and I said 'I haven't got a group', and I remember everyone turned around to stare. I was looking at one of my friends who was mouthing, 'I'm so sorry.' It was so exposing and awful. The trainer said, 'You need to choose.' And I said, 'I can't! – Don't ask me to choose between one side or the other because I am both of them – I AM MIXED! Here is my group – I am in the middle!' and I just stayed there and refused to move.

Laila Woozeer, whose voice has been present throughout this book in the many media articles they have contributed to expanding the mixed and multiracial dialogue in the mainstream, is also author of the stunning memoir *Not Quite White* that takes us on a 'meta magical realism' journey through their life, using visual symbols and motifs to navigate their mixed identity experience. Their book describes someone who has integrated and even *alchemised* their mixed experience, despite the racial bullying and turmoil they went through. Laila also demonstrates a remarkable resilience in the face of intergenerational trauma by dismantling the heaviness of the topic with a dreamlike style of storytelling using the symbols of a leopard and a tiger, to convey their colonised indentured slavery lineage.

> I wanted it to be almost like intergenerational trauma is almost like a character or a force that appears in this book. I started thinking a bit in terms of sort of other genres, you know, like in a fantasy novel or something, you've

got like an enemy that comes in and out. I thought, how do you visualise intergenerational trauma? And I thought – with these two cats circling each other, out to fight!

ENHANCED CREATIVITY, ADAPTABILITY + OPEN-MINDEDNESS

In an article called 'The biracial advantage' for *Psychology Today*, writer Jennifer Latson says, 'What gives multiracial people a creative edge may simply be that they have more practice navigating between multiple identities.'[7] This echoes what I mentioned earlier, that our experience of navigating mixed life with multiple lenses may actually *help* us develop these skills. As Latson continues, 'Being around multiracial people can boost creativity and agile thinking for monoracials too, according to research by University of Hawaii psychologist Kristin Pauker.'

As someone with an art background, Clara is contemplative about how being mixed has impacted her creativity:

I feel like it gives a bit more of an interesting process when it comes to self-discovery, because I feel creativity is an expression of self. From my experience of being mixed, I have really struggled with my identity, and, who I am, I feel like I don't fit in – with a group of white people, I'm seen as Black, and in a group of Black people I'm seen as 'mixed race' or just not Black, basically. So I think that has kind of informed my creativity and my art in kind of posing that question: 'Who am I?; What do I look like?' And those are actually questions that I reflect on often, because, you know, that lack of identity is kind of a hindrance over me, so I feel like it makes me go inwards, or makes me need to go inwards to remind myself of who I am. Because sometimes on the outside, it doesn't feel very obvious, if that makes sense?

Although it might stem from a certain distress, travelling inwards is the aspect that ultimately helps Clara's creative process:

If I spend a bit of time on an art journal, that, for me, allows me to feel more centred and kind of come back into myself. Because sometimes, when you're, you know, in society you're being projected onto, as something or someone that maybe you don't feel you are, it can have an impact. So, you know, I know who I am, and it's just nice to have a creative practice that allows me to be reminded of that from time to time.

I'm of the firm belief that every human being is potentially creative, but perhaps seeking an outlet to express ourselves (out of sheer necessity) combined with the unique way in which mixed people so often do express ourselves (without following the same rules as everyone else) might actually benefit us in more ways than we realise. Mixed and multiracial people also sometimes don't feel the same loyalty to behaving in a certain way to fit in with a specific group, which could help us be more innovative because it allows more unrestricted freedom to try new things that then utilise our well-practised outside-the-box thinking. Laila runs Not Quite Night, a community circle for mixed creatives, and they also feel mixed creativity comes down to a sense of freedom that we have lived and practised, from being on the margins.

Mixed people never had that structure anyway, so we're OK to lose it! We've had to construct something from 'somewhere' in the first place. I've gone through that, and then I've come out of it. So whatever happens, it's like – I'm fine! I can do that. I know I can do that!! But some people have never had that [lack of blueprint] tested. They're in whatever 'mould' they began in, and the idea of losing that structure and having to build something new scares them.

Kyley from Chapters 3 and 6 says:

My creativity may have developed in childhood from a need to invent an identity for myself, as society had not created one for me. With no concrete narrative available of who I am and what I am supposed to be, there is great freedom. My culture is made up of many parts of global cultures, and I feel empowered to access them all and synthesise art in new and unexpected ways. As a global citizen – from everywhere and yet from nowhere – I have the freedom to express myself without limitations.

This mixed and multiracial creative liberation is also embodied by Isamnu Noguchi, one of the 20th century's most critically acclaimed artists. Noguchi (Japanese and white American) is described by leading contemporary gallery White Cube as 'an itinerant cultural synthesizer' who 'consistently rejected categorization and the false dichotomies of his time.'[8] Noguchi used his entire art career to explore and escape from many of the struggles he faced about his mixedness, focusing on truly making the most of his expansive identity, embodying multifaceted mixed creativity in his lifetime. The website Mixed Race Studies says, 'During his sixty-year career, there was hardly a genre that Noguchi failed to explore. He produced more than 2,500 works of sculpture, designed furniture, lamps, and stage sets, created dramatic public gardens all over the world, and pioneered the development of environmental art...' expressing the sheer magnitude of Noguchi's creative expression.[9]

DEEPENED EMPATHY + GENUINE UNDERSTANDING FOR OTHERS, ESPECIALLY THOSE WITH DIFFERENCE

In an interview for BBC4, *Biracial Britain* author Remi Adekoya says, 'The good thing very often about people who are biracial or multiracial is they've come into contact with people from different ethnic or racial groups, and can form a more sort of kinder opinion about humanity.'[10] Mixed people may have developed a lot of empathy, understanding and compassion for others, due to having learnt to feel into so many different racial, cultural and opposing perspectives in our lives. Clara shares:

> *I do feel like I have a lot of patience. And that is mainly because of my dad. He learned English when he was 25, whilst I was growing up – my dad didn't really have great English. So I I think it's given me a bit more perspective and awareness for those that are coming from non-speaking English countries, and I feel more empathy for people like that, because I've seen how my dad has struggled and survived and thrived through an environment that kind of discourages you if you have an accent, or if learning English is very challenging. So I feel like, for people that don't understand English, I'm really, really patient.*

Allyson (who you met in Chapter 3) says:

> *I think it's part of what makes me a good therapist, because I can be sitting with someone from a completely different background, and I can usually still find some way of connection. I can understand why you did this, or why you thought that. There's like, a different level of empathy, I think.*

Aware of how racially polarised the world is becoming, Allyson says:

> *I think it's interesting how right now, we're so divided with race. Mixed race people have this unique positionality of, like, sort of being a bridge between cultures. If I take the white side of me and the Mexican side, there's a lot of racial trauma between those groups. But as mixed race we are sort of this bridge that I think is vital! We need more of that for us all to become more united I think as humans. I have friends from every different background, and again, I can always find that connection piece.*

A UNIQUE LENS IN LOVE, FRIENDSHIP + RELATIONSHIPS

'When identities cross boundaries, love knows no bounds' reads the rousing statement from Ismée Amiel Williams and Rebecca Balcárcel in the book *Boundless: Twenty Voices Celebrating Multicultural and Multiracial Identities*. The book explores stories celebrating mixed love and relationship dynamics and suggests that in being mixed, we bring a unique perspective: 'Because we have lived in two or more cultures we have also developed extraordinary empathy and resilience. We recognize multiple ways of living, multiple lenses on the world, and various sides of conversations because we live, speak and breathe these different sides.'[11] Being mixed means we do have tremendous capacity for love across difference, again because we have been navigating this racial and cultural multiplicity within ourselves and all around us since our birth, and it's what feels practised and familiar.

Although it is entirely possible for any person to be prejudiced, holding prejudice is in direct opposition to our inherent state of existing as multiracial people. If mixed people embody multiple races, how can it then make sense for us to then be against ourselves or any side of our family? I believe that in our highest version of ourselves, mixed people are in closer proximity (through our experience of our family dynamics) to seeing people of all races as true equals. As the mixed Japanese American artist Isamu Noguchi wrote in his 1942 essay: 'To be hybrid anticipates the future... The racial and cultural intermixture is the antithesis of all the tenets of the Axis Powers. For us to fall into the Fascist line of race bigotry is to defeat our unique personality and strength.'[12]

After all, despite the challenges, we have also seen what IS possible beyond the boundaries of race and culture, from watching our own parents' unique interracial dynamics. We also have a unique 'insider's view' of each group in relation to one another – both positive *and* negative. 'I feel like I have a very realistic view about everyone that isn't based upon a myopic view of the world,'[13] says one anonymous contributor on mixedremixed.org, implying that mixed people have learnt to be discerning towards all groups, and with that maybe have developed a more honest view than how those groups might sometimes see themselves.

You might also be attached to some highly specific relational traits that are unique to your mum and dad's combined interracial relationship, that shaped how you come to love and express love. For example, my parents were communicating in a third language that was foreign to both of them, so maybe in a bid to make up for what was lost in translation, they made an effort to bond over their shared humour a lot, which is something I really value too! For those who try to dictate to mixed and multiracial people who they should date, they might do well to remember we are born from a combination of two or more different races ourselves, so what makes sense to them might not feel the same to us! In 'Biracial dating in a monoracial culture', for *Psychology Today*, therapist Tiffany Mclain says there is a unique lens that biracial people bring to the dating world.[14] She points out that there are challenges mixed people face because they might see things a bit differently to monoracial people due to being racially non-binary. But as with everything else about the duality of being mixed, regardless of difficulties, there is also splendour in the way we see things, which will also uniquely impact relationships.

'I am a product of a mixed race marriage, and so I see the beauty of going outside of just what you always know, if that's something that you prefer to do. As long as you're willing to make it work,' says Cedric Stout (Black American and Korean heritage) on *The Halfie Project*, a podcast he co-presents with Becky, his mixed Korean and white partner.[15]

Cedric says he is very aware of some of the perceptions others might have about who he dates and that he deeply empathises with why they might think like that, but his different outlook, due to being multiracial, must be respected:

It's just an interesting place to be in, because there's different perspectives that I've seen – none of them are incorrect. And it's like, if I choose one, then, you know, people of the other perspectives may have an issue with that. At the end of the day, I can't be bothered by the opinions of everybody, because you can't satisfy everybody.

He reiterates that who we love as mixed people, just like how we might choose to identify, is specific to our own life experience and is *our* choice!

WE CAN MERGE WITH MANY DIFFERENT GROUPS

Even though we don't fit into any one group specifically, we also can *shapeshift* in many groups due to our ambiguity and multiplicity, as Clara mentioned earlier. Our exposure to so many cultures means we are often comfortable going between various cultures and races and might not feel uncomfortable in the way monoracial people can be more prone to, due to not being raised with multiracial non-binary duality and multiplicity.

Laila has also noticed that mixed people have developed harmonisation skills that allow us to diplomatically surf between opposing perspectives.

I think that one thing that I've seen in the research that really resonated with me was, mixed race people tend to be more agreeable in seeing different points of views. Because, we've been navigating family systems where there's maybe clashing cultural views, religious views, and like, we can hold multiple truths easier than someone without that experience.

This mixed talent for maintaining and navigating challenging intercultural diplomatic relations across countries is something that also becomes an asset in business. In the book *On Managing Across Cultures* for *Harvard Business Review* by Erin Meyer, Hal B Gregersen, Jeanne Brett and Yves Dozit, it was reported that 'Multicultural managers have frequently defused acrimonious communications between a subsidiary and L'Oréal Paris.'[16] The team leaders' mixed Indian-American-French heritage possessed a nuanced cultural understanding that was effective in helping smooth out misunderstandings between the French team and the Indian team. The book noted the mixed team leader was highly attuned to the lack of collaboration that was causing a rupture between the teams, allowing them to 'decode each other's [differing cultural] expressions of expectations'.

'I always felt like, when you're mixed, you know how to flow in a space,' says Sophie Kanno, who you met in Chapters 1, 2 and 4. Sophie, who grew up in the US, is Japanese mixed herself. 'We grew up around a lot of Black and brown people, a lot of kids who were immigrants, people from Haiti, lots of Cape Verdeans, lots of Puerto Ricans, Dominicans, Filipinos and Chinese. But there weren't many Japanese people.' She explains how her mixed empathy helps her to blend in groups when everyone is different from each other, because she *knows* how it feels to be culturally alone and she doesn't want others to feel like that. 'You can find the connections somehow, because no one has ever been like you either, or has your story.'

Take a moment

- Consider how you might 'think outside the box' and how it's been beneficial to your life and well-being.
- Can you think of a time when your multiple mixed lens has helped you in your life, work or creativity?
- What is your relationship with your duality and multiplicity? How has it been an advantage for you personally?
- Do you give yourself permission to acknowledge your strengths and resilience? What are the ways in which you demonstrate your strength?
- Do you acknowledge your creativity? Why or why not? Is it easy or hard for you to access? How would you like to develop this in the future?

REFLECTION

1. What comes up for you about celebrating yourself for being mixed?
2. Have you ever considered that you might possess mixed superpowers in this way?
3. List your mixed talents and reflect on how they personally help you in your life.

Chapter 11

Creating your own culture + building legacy

CELEBRATING BEING MIXED +
MULTIRACIAL ON OUR OWN TERMS!

> *Namazonia! It's the place to be*
> *Namazonia! You can climb the trees*
> *Namazonia! It's the place to be*
> *Namazonia! Let yourself be free!*
> 'NAMAZONIA', NAMALEE BOLLE

Discovering there is no blueprint for being mixed and multiracial is certainly a dilemma, but it also presents us with an opportunity for immense self-realisations. When you are the only one who can create the way forward for yourself and you find yourself without a map, instructions or leaders to follow, you might find yourself conforming to how things should look rather than re-imagining how they could look. Forging your own path when there's no guidebook and trying to move towards finding peace and fulfilment in the life *between the borderlands* can be its own precious gift, especially if we think of ourselves as our own identity pioneers buccaneering and swashbuckling our way towards a brand new *fusion territory*!

As journalist Joel Cotkin wrote for *Forbes*, 'In the current world, being a "race of races" represents not a dissolution of power, but a new means for expressing it.'[1] How then, might a new expression of mixed power look to you personally? How might it appear to your senses: taste, sight, smell, sound and touch? Shifting our perspective away from the binary mindset, we might start to reconsider what we have gained rather than over-focusing on what has been culturally lacking in our experience. We may not have understood the languages around us as a child, but maybe we developed extra sensory skills from reading facial expressions and hearing vocal tones to understand others instead. That is a gift in itself that might help someone communicate better with neurodivergent people and differently abled friends and acquaintances.

The liminal space can become something to reclaim, to set up a whole life in! A homely bridge between cultural worlds, itself becoming a place that feels authentic to rest our head, at long last! If we consider ourselves to be *both* or *all* rather than desolate lonely bits and pieces endlessly searching, this naturally lends itself to truly enjoying our beautiful fusions; whether it be with our food, our style or other modes of multicultural self-expression! In her book *Borderlands/La Fronteria: The New Mestiza*, queer feminist Chicana writer Gloria Anzaldúa developed her own theories about living inside marginal worlds. She wrote her seminal book in both English and Spanish prose to make a point about purposefully living at the crossroads and contemplating the mixing of cultures that developed along the borders from her own life of being born on the Mexico/US border: 'To live in the Borderlands', she writes, 'means to put chilie in the borscht, eat whole wheat tortillas, speak Tex-Mex with a Brooklyn accent.'

Firmly and defiantly planting ourselves in the spirit of embracing our contradictions, mixed and multiracial people can also start to ask ourselves where we can begin to weave together *all* of our aspects, with a lot more gusto! Thinking about the different facets of your personal culture might also mean a remixing of what you understood before, a uniquely curated mixture of all your influences together, in the way *only you* see things.

Don't be afraid to mix whatever you want in there too. Whatever feels culturally relevant to you can go straight into the creative pot! Nora Fakim is a BBC reporter of Moroccan Mauritian-Indian heritage who created a beautiful series of 'mixed boxes'[2] She asked several people to each fill a box with a mixture of meaningful artefacts that represented their mixed heritage.[3] Devon Fisher-Aziz (Pakistani and English) included some elephant ornaments, a St Christopher's cross, a Spice Girls 'Girl Power' book and some South Asian bangles, whilst Ethan Boachie-Barrance (Ghanaian and English) included his great-grandmother's Kente cloth, a toy underground tube train, a notepad and a pen from his Ghanaian grandmother... You get the picture – *now go make your own version!* Nostalgic symbols, cultural trinkets and artefacts go a long way to connecting us with our deeper selves, evoking memories that go beyond language and speech straight to the unconscious self. These objects can awaken sensory parts that connect us ancestrally, spiritually and nostalgically, in a way that speaking often can't. Don't overthink it – collect and assemble what feels instinctive!

You can choose whichever medium you prefer to unlock the various cultural narratives inside you. I like to work visually and also equally as much with the written word. No artistic restrictions for me! My 'Namazonia' lyrics in the epigraph are from a song I wrote in 2006, where I decided to reclaim all the parts of my mixed identity as its own island – re-imagining it as a nation in itself with its own values, rules and cultural beliefs that were different from any country I had known before.

Playing around and experimenting with your own cultural signatures might start somewhere like creating your very own mixed box of artefacts, like Nora Fakim did, or experimenting with cooking and remembering recipes that your family made. Ask your family members to write down a load of recipes so that you can delight in learning them and can pass them down too. If this is not possible for you, even just finding recipes yourself that are connected with your various cultures or creating your own cultural rituals with them can be great as well!

Semra Haksever aka MamaMoon is an author, eclectic witch and intuitive healer of Turkish-Cypriot and Polish heritage, who has always felt a longing to create her *own* culture. 'I think it's because of the lack of being part of any kind of group, like, growing up always feeling very much like a Londoner, but not having any firm Turkish or Polish roots, because we didn't grow up in communities with those people,' Semra says. 'My mum's family are all Polish and blonde. On a psychological level, I realise now that I was the black sheep. I'm physically so different from them.'

Semra also had to reckon with two different religious influences, mixing separately at different times in her identity development.

My dad was kind of a 'cherry-picking Muslim' but he was very big on his Turkish culture: Turkish music, everything Turkish! He was really patriotic. And then he left, when I was 11 and my mum had a huge bout of Catholic guilt, because she'd been brought up a strict Catholic, and she immediately took us to church.

Creating her own 'combination culture' through witchcraft and drawing from all of her heritages has made Semra feel totally immersed in herself and who she is.

> *There's a certain element of being able to create my own traditions and my own cultures that have made me feel quite rooted. Maybe I haven't done it consciously. When I look back, I'm like, 'Ah, these things are a longing!' I'm inviting these rituals into my life, or having something that gives me this sense of belonging on the planet. And I think that witchcraft is definitely something that's kind of given me that kind of identity, or an identity made from my own kind of traditions, my own rituals. It gives me a sense of security.*

FOOD AS A SACRED PORTAL OF CULTURAL CONNECTION

Those of us from mixed backgrounds have often grown up with food as a strong symbol of love and connection to our culture, because, well, food can't be escaped! Black and Brown parents often nurture us through their joy in feeding us! Even if we haven't been taught our parents' or families' languages, they likely did feed us at least some of our original cultural cuisine. They often feed us very well too – with food being a love language and a unifying part of our cultures and traditions with the idiosyncratic combos of food we eat often becoming a defining part of our mixed experience. As poet Dean Atta (who is British Jamaican and Greek Cypriot) wrote in his poem 'I Come From': 'I come from shepherds pie and Sunday roast, Jerk chicken and stuffed vine leaves, I come from travelling through my taste buds but loving where I live'.[4]

Have you also noticed how many avant-garde chefs are also from mixed and multiracial backgrounds?! Scully, St James in London is the brainchild of Malaysian-born Chinese-Indian and Irish-Balinese Ramael Scully who grew up in Sydney, Australia. Scully's innovative menu includes eccentrically eclectic dishes that purposefully mix unique ingredients from all over the world in awe-inspiring, daring combinations like their steamed sea bass drizzled in Ethiopian spice-butter, salt-brined green tomatillos lightly pickled in apple vinegar and pastrami spice and potatoes served with Irish samphire. And celebrity chef Molly Yeh told *The Jewish Womens Archive*: 'My pops is Chinese and my mum is New York (but before that, Hungarian)! I'm Chinese and Jewish. I celebrate Christmas, Hanukkah, and three New Years, and I like pastrami in my egg rolls!'[5]

Naturally for Semra, cooking is an important aspect of connecting with her mixedness: 'I know that these simple dishes I make have probably just been eaten in my family for years. I do think about my ancestors a lot when I eat and when I'm cooking.' She says, 'Being really present in your senses feels like something important – like smell, you know how you burn stuff and you're eating and, you know, touching different things connecting with it all.'

My mum's love language is most certainly food as well and making the most delicious dishes anyone has ever tasted is her terrain! From Sri Lankan fish curries, rice hoppers, prawn sambals and *Wattalapan* to spag bol, homemade chocolate mousse and Dutch *hutspot* – there isn't a dish on earth my mum hasn't attempted to supply us with her whole heart. For children of South Asian mothers, cutting up fruit (particularly mangoes) lovingly delivered to our bedrooms as a teenager is a rite of passage! As an adult I cherish when I go to her house and she cuts fruit for me – it feels so special and so connecting! On my other side, Dutch *haring* and *patat met frites saus* topped off with an ice cool can of *Chocomel* bought from an Amsterdam street vendor has the power to send me into floods of tears. Such is the sacred connection to my beloved *Oma*, who I mostly knew also through food and our shopping trips to the Dutch supermarket chain *Albert Heijn*. Even going on a pilgrimage to the supermarket just to inhale the *brood* (bread), *vriend mosselen* (fried mussels) and *Ontbijtkoek* (Dutch honey cake) can feel like an almost religious experience for mixed and multiracial people!

Create your own mixed memory recipe

- Think about some meals you ate growing up on both/ all sides of your family that you would like to recreate. Which ones did you like best and why?

- Ask family or caregivers for recipes or write down any you can remember.
- Think about the aromatic resonance and what memories each dish might evoke for you.
- Choose one or two recipes to recreate yourself, taking time to savour the experience.

CONNECTING WITH AROMATIC MEMORIES OF MIXEDNESS

Smells trigger nostalgia and memory, maybe more than any other sense, time-travelling to take us beyond words and sometimes beyond pain too, because when we inhale aromas during childhood they are processed by a part of the limbic system – the olfactory bulb, one of the first parts of the brain to develop in childhood.

'My one happy memory of my dad was that we had a jasmine bush, and he'd pick the jasmine and he'd make me little flower crowns with it,' remembers Semra. 'When I was in Italy a few weeks ago, there was this jasmine bush outside our Airbnb! And every night me and my friend would literally just stick our heads in the bush like, it smells so good! It was so powerful!' The jasmine scent evoked a loving memory of Semra's father.

I know that my dad loved jasmine because that reminded him of his time in Cyprus. I haven't got the best relationship with my dad, but I know when I was smelling the jasmine, I was having that thought of like, this reaction to the jasmine isn't my reaction alone – it's in my DNA, it's in my hippocampus!

The thoughts conjure family members from many generations ago:

Great, great, great grandmothers would probably sniff in the jasmine as a simple pleasure and it was probably making them so happy!! And I'm here and it is making ME so happy! This divine scent!! There is some kind of memory that it's invoking here.

EXPRESSING YOUR MIXEDNESS
THROUGH FASHION + STYLE

Both Semra and myself are ex-fashion editors and have often discussed how we were both drawn to clothing as a way of expressing our multicultural heritages, and *still* are! As a forever fashion enthusiast, I have learnt that you can paint pictures with clothes, using the garments themselves to tell cultural narratives, interweaving symbolic accessories to represent multicultural identity and traditions about your own heritage. Fuschia pink is known as the navy blue of South Asia, so naturally bright, vibrant colours laden with armfuls of maximalist bangles became my signature style.

'Fashion is a vital part of my self-expression,' says Roxanne, aka the Multiple Sclerosis Fashionista.

> *I attended an Irish school but also experienced a very Caribbean upbringing in my daily life. It was peak garage music era, so much of my free time was spent at the local estate park with friends, listening to people spin records and spit bars. Barbecues and dinners at my Nan's house were always filled with soca music and joyful dancing – it was beautiful! My style is a reflection of my heritage, my upbringing, and the things that bring me joy. I gravitate toward bold, vivid colours, influenced by the vibrant Caribbean aesthetics and 90s fashion of my childhood.*

Roxanne stylishly mixes all aspects of her intersectional identity to make a sartorial statement:

> *Even my mobility aids have become part of my style. A beautifully designed walking stick shifts the narrative from 'What's wrong with you?' to 'Where did you get that?' Fashion gives me the power to shape how I'm perceived and opens doors to conversations about my intersecting identities.*

Having fun and being playful with your cultural clothing is how I encourage you to try things out when considering how to express your own mixed heritage through your style! Becoming more connected to our own multicultural heritage clothing culture is distinctly personal, but it's something we can all experiment with – whether you are a vintage queen, an avid minimalist or maybe you prefer something altogether more formal? You can even try mixing your traditional cultural styles from both sides together with more modern pieces as an experiment.

'I deserve to wear a Dirndl as much as I deserve to wear a traditional carnival costume' posted Mixed Girl Meetup's Shakayra Stern on her Instagram.[6] 'What I continue to realise is that at every Mixed Girl Meetup I organise, showing up as our authentic selves, whether that's in a Dashiki, a Dirndl or a saree or just plain jeans and a T-shirt, is an immensely healing act in itself,' she says.

'These pieces of clothing – they're our memories. They are the fabric of our lives and what we do with them is our legacy!' says Emma Slade Edmondson, *The Half of It* author and *Mixed Up* podcaster in her TedX Talk 'The Fabric of Life', where the sustainability consultant discusses the depth of her relationship with clothing as symbolic artefacts of her life, especially after her mother's passing in her twenties.[7] 'This is my nan's skirt,' says Emma, about the gorgeous mid-length pleated number she is wearing. 'She wore it to my mum's wedding, to her golden wedding anniversary and to my wedding, and now I'm wearing it because I am my mother's daughter, and she was my nan's daughter and I want you to know them,' showing how meaningful it feels to tell a story about our family through what we wear and how it is styled.

The mixed styling challenge

- Design a look from items in your wardrobe – mixed with a few traditional pieces that are borrowed from your parents/grandparents/relatives, etc. – that combine all your cultural heritages and style influences together. If this is not possible, find some items in charity shops or borrow items from friends that represent your different cultures.

- Don't forget accessories too – a pair of your auntie's golden jhumka earrings or your granny's cowry shell necklace can really make or break a look!

- Create a narrative about how you want to style and express this outfit in your fashion story and find a location that feels relevant to your cultural heritage that you can use as a backdrop. You could even use some draped sari fabric, lace or batik printed cloth (or use your culture's equivalent) as an indoor background.

- You can either model the outfit yourself, or ask a friend to model it for you and take photos to document your mixed inspired outfit.

EXPLORING THE *SOUND* OF MIXED IDENTITY

Daren Banarsë is a composer and music therapist of Indian and Irish heritage who has taken things to the next level. He decided to build his own 'mixed race inspired musical instrument' – that he named the Unola (from Onus in Latin meaning 'one') – to discover the actual sound of his mixedness! 'It sounds like a mix between an accordion and a harmonica, with a sweet tone,' says Daren. 'It's a sound that sits remarkably well within many genres – especially Irish and Indian. In Irish music it sounds like the Irish concertina, and in Indian music it sounds like the Indian harmonium.'

For his research MA, Daren was tasked with creating an auto-ethnography (an academic autobiography about your own culture):

As part of my identity, I've often wondered what sort of music I should be playing? I'm attracted to all sorts of different music and I was like, 'I want to celebrate my mixed race musicality.' So rather than 'fight against the system', my way of going about things is to see what I've got and make something original with that.

Daren was already an expert at building melodicas (a kind of handheld free-reed instrument that looks like a mini organ), so he just thought he would experiment and see what happens.

Ideally, it would be an instrument that I would make my own music on, and it might reflect that I love Irish music and also that I love Indian music, and a lot of music from England as well. And I thought, why not make an instrument which might reflect all of these cultures?

Daren sourced Irish cattle bones and ebony wood from India to get started on his mixed musical masterpiece. He recognised that being born in London was also an essential part of his mixed identity and he needed to add that element too, so he made the casing from some timber that was sourced from a fallen tree in Soho Square. 'I have a long history with Soho Square, because after Saturday music college, I used to visit it. It's the sort of place you know as a Londoner – with the Indian fair trust run by Harry Krishnas and Ronnie Scott's around the corner – and Maison Bertaux!'

With its black *major* keys and white *minor* keys and multisided hexagonal beige casing, the Unola seems to really reflect something about Daren's own phenotype whilst also reflecting some of the mixed and multiracial qualities we spoke about last chapter. 'The versatility of sound wasn't something I expected, but it really adds to the flexibility of the Unola. Just like I'm part of three distinct cultures, the instrument effortlessly improvises within the music of whatever cultural context it finds itself,' he says proudly.

Flying the mixed and multiracial 'flag of your personal 'mixedness''!

Nations, tribes and clans declare themselves and their identity with flags, insignia, tribal fabric patterns, coats of arms and heraldry. This is your opportunity to re-imagine how a 'flag of your personal 'mixedness'' might appear.

You will need:

Two paper straws

Sellotape

Scissors

White A4 paper

Magazines to collage

Colouring pens

- You can incorporate anything you like into your flag as an expression of your personal and unique mixed identity. Look out for imagery that connects with all aspects of who you are from the multiracial, to cultural, to other intersections that relate to your full identity.

- Bond the two straws together with reinforced tape and then fasten your A4 paper flag to the upper section with another strip of tape. Now you are ready to decorate your 'flag of self'. Use collage and anything else you want to draw to symbolise the 'land of yourself' through your own imagery.

- Take your time to create your work and place your 'flag of self' in your window when it's finished, so the world can witness your mixed and multiracial pride!

Chapter 12

Exercises + resources

FURTHER SUPPORT FROM MIXED PRACTITIONERS

EXERCISE 1: WELLBEING TRIANGLE FOR REFLECTIONS ON BEING MIXED AND MULTIRACIAL

By Dr Mish Seabrook
(www.michelleseabrook.co.uk; Instagram @drmishseabrook)

Consider these three aspects of your mixed well-being: physical, psychological and spiritual Use the prompts below to think about the amount of focus you currently place on each. For each of the three sections draw a separate triangle to imagine how you balance these 3 sides e.g. Physical Wellbeing triangle: Side 1 Body awareness; Side 2 Health; Side 3 Nutrition and diet, etc. What would each triangle look like? There is no right or wrong triangle, it's just about noticing the difference in each side. Are there some areas of your wellbeing you think about a lot compared to others? Do you notice any areas which need more attention?

Physical well-being

Side 1. Body awareness
- How do you feel about your physical appearance as a mixed individual?
- In what ways do you feel your mixed culture influences your physical health and fitness practices?
- How do you practise body positivity and compassion?

Side 2. Health
- What health practices from your cultures do you incorporate into your life?
- Are there any physical activities or sports that make you feel more connected to being mixed?

Side 3. Nutrition and diet
- How do you connect with and include foods from your mixed cultural backgrounds into your diet?
- Are there any family recipes or traditional dishes that you find particularly nourishing, both physically and emotionally?

Psychological well-being

1. Identity and self-concept
   - How do you describe your mixed race identity to yourself and others, and how does it impact on your sense of self?
   - What aspects of your identity bring you the most pride and joy?

2. Emotional resilience
   - Reflect on a time when you faced a challenge related to your mixed race identity. How did you overcome it?
   - What coping strategies have you developed to deal with difficult emotions or experiences?
   - What self-care (e.g. therapy, journaling, meditation) do you find most beneficial?

3. Support
   - Who are the key people in your life that support your mental well-being and understanding of your mixed race identity?
   - How can you strengthen and expand your support network?

Spiritual well-being

1. Cultural and spiritual traditions
   - Which spiritual or cultural traditions from your heritage do you find most meaningful?
   - How do you include these traditions in your daily life?

2. Sense of belonging
   - How does your mixed identity influence your sense of belonging in various spiritual or religious communities?
   - Which practices help you feel spiritually grounded and connected to your history?

3. Purpose and meaning
   - How does your mixed race identity shape your sense of purpose and meaning in life?

– Which spiritual or philosophical beliefs guide you through challenges and uncertainties?

Further reflections

Think on the following:

- What insights did you gain about your physical, psychological and
  spiritual well-being?
- How did these reflections impact your daily life and sense of self?
- What areas do you feel need more attention or exploration?
- What commitment can you make to address the areas that need
  more exploration?

EXERCISE 2: MEDITATION FOR EMBRACING YOUR MIXED + MULTIRACIAL IDENTITY

By Allyson Inez Ford (Instagram @bodyjusticetherapist)

You might like to ask a trusted mixed friend to read this aloud for you whilst you partake in the exercise:

- Begin by bringing your attention into your body.
- You can close your eyes or keep them slightly open – the most important thing is that you are comfortable.
- Take a moment to notice your body's weight wherever you're seated, feeling the weight of your body on the chair, on the floor, on your bed. Feel how the earth is supporting you.
- Take a few deep breaths, in through your nose and out through your mouth.
- Visualise your ancestors, all who came before you, standing behind you. (You might not know how they look so you might just see them as colour or energies.) Feel their strength and warmth embracing you. Visualise the future generations in front of you – looking to you for guidance and love.
- And as you take a deep breath, bring in more oxygen, enlivening the body. And as you exhale, have a sense of relaxing more deeply.
- Feel in your body that you are enough, just as you are. Feel that you are worthy and whole just as you are.
- You are on the difficult but rewarding journey of understanding your mixed race experience more fully. Many of us grew up without a sense of true belonging, our identity in the eyes of the beholder. This can leave us feeling unseen; it can leave us with sadness and self-doubt.
- Notice whatever feelings arise when you think about your mixed race experience, identify where you feel this in your body.
- Breathe in this feeling. Breathe in the pain, sadness or isolation. Breathe out the opposite, breathe out comfort, peace and community.
- Set your intention on how you would like to embrace your mixed race experience going forward, and how you can integrate self-trust, self-validation and empowerment into your life.

- Breathe in all the difficult feelings and memories that all of the mixed race people in the world deal with every day; and then breathe out peace, calmness and community for us all.
- Imagine a world where we are all embraced and seen for exactly who we are – with all of our unique challenges and struggles, we are enough.
- We don't need to justify our existence or ethnicity to anyone, because we know in our hearts exactly who we are. No one can take that from us.
- We can imagine the strength of our ancestors and remember that even if we don't know them, they are with us. Even if we have never visited our motherlands, those places are imprinted in our hearts and souls. We are never alone.
- We are not half or a quarter of anything – we are whole, we can choose to identify as we please. We can choose who to share our stories with. We can choose how we show up in this world.
- Breathe in deep; and exhale. Feel the weight of your body again. Notice your feet on the floor. Notice your back on the chair. Notice your jaw, your neck, let out a big sigh and sink into your body. Be aware of your whole body as best you can. Take a breath. And then when you're ready, you can open your eyes.

EXERCISE 3: REFLECTING ON YOUR PAST + PRESENT

By Alex Lewis

(www.riseuptherapy.com; Instagram @riseuptherapyservice)

What did it mean to be Black/brown growing up? (3 words/sentences)

. . . .

What did it mean to be 'mixed race' growing up? (3 words/sentences)

. . . .

What did it mean to be 'white' growing up? (3 words/sentences)

. . . .

What parts of you existed in all three? (3 words/sentences)

. . . .

Write a little about what came up for you when it comes to what it meant to be Black/white/mixed growing up

. . . .

. . . .

. . . .

. . . .

What does it mean to be Black/brown now? (3 words/sentences)

. . . .

What does it mean to be 'mixed race' now? (3 words/sentences

. . . .

What does it mean to be 'white' now? (3 words/sentences)

. . . .

What parts of you exist in all three now? (3 words/sentences)

. . . .

Write a little about what came up for you when you think about what it means to be Black/white/mixed now

....

....

....

....

Ask yourself how you experienced your mixedness at each age period and the feelings you had

5–10 years old

....

10–20 years old

....

20–30 years old

....

30+ years old

....

EXERCISE 4: YOUR TRANSPERSONAL HAIR DIARY

By Jamila Andersson (rememberwhowearetherapy.com)

You will need a sketchbook or scrapbook that you can dedicate to your hair story to journal, draw and stick pictures and photos.

Hair is believed to enhance a person's 'antenna ability'. This ability allows individuals to connect with their spiritual side and develop higher levels of consciousness that go beyond the ego. Developing and embracing your natural hair growth deepens spiritual connections. It honours our ancestral heritage and unites mixed race individuals with divine forces.

1. Explore your beliefs about your hair in your diary. Where did these beliefs come from? Are they positive or negative? Do they empower you or hold you back? Understanding these beliefs is a crucial step towards developing a healthy and positive relationship with your mixed race hair. Take some time to journal on what comes up for you. Spend as long as you need and update whenever you feel the need, adding photos or drawings of your feelings towards your hair.

2. Draw a timeline of your hair from birth to now. Add in significant and memorable moments, making a note of your relationship to your hair at the time. Think about discovering your hair texture and comments that people made about it.

3. Research each of your specific heritages' spiritual beliefs about hair. Hair is spiritual in a myriad of ways. Several cultures have viewed hair as a source of strength, including one of the earliest descriptions in the Bible of Samson's hair symbolising his connection to divine power.

You might consider:

*   Afro-textured hair grows in a helix shape, symbolising strength, authenticity and strong will. For thousands of years, African hair has been considered sacred. It serves as a beacon of spirituality, allowing a connection to divine forces and an otherworldly realm.

- Native Americans view hair as a source of power and spiritual connection. Uncut hair is an antenna linking them to the spirit world, ancestors and natural elements. Long hair symbolises wisdom, strength and reverence for all life.

- Sikhs maintain uncut hair (known as Kesh) as a sacred practice. It's seen as a gift from God, reflecting the commitment to faith, identity and spiritual connection.

- Rastafarians wear dreadlocks as a spiritual practice. It connects them to Africa, their culture and spiritual consciousness. Dreadlocks represent naturalness, purity and adherence to Rastafarian principles.

4. Think about how you can develop your own unique hair rituals that resonate with you to help you carry spiritual significance and connect you to your roots.

Remember, these practices demonstrate how hair transcends mere aesthetics – they carry spiritual, cultural and social weight, shaping our identities and connecting us to our roots.

EXERCISE 5: REMEMBERING + REDISCOVERING YOUR AUTHENTIC MIXED VOICE

By Jasmin Harsono (www.emeraldandtiger. com; @emeraldandtiger)

I invite you to delve into the power of breath, movement, humming, intuitive sounding and silence, followed by some reflective journaling prompts. I suggest reading through each section, practising them individually and then integrating them into a full-bodied practice that you can engage in daily or whenever you feel called. Remember, your sounding voice is medicine for the heart and soul. Take your time with this practice. Honour how you feel and what your practice looks like now. Remember, there is no right or wrong way to do this. Allow yourself to be in the now and embrace the journey as it unfolds.

Breath
You can find a comfortable seated position or stand with your feet firmly planted. Feel your body rooting to the floor, grounding into the earth. Safely close your eyes or keep them open and take a deep breath through your nose, allowing your belly, diaphragm, chest, lungs and whole body to expand fully. Exhale slowly through your mouth, sighing, releasing tension or stress. Repeat this process several times, focusing on the sensation of your breath filling your body. Imagine breathing into your body and grounding into the earth and all around the universe and all loved ones. Continue to breathe and repeat the words: I am safe; I am not alone; I am supported; I am whole.

Movement
Begin by moving your body in a manner that feels natural and liberating. Engage in gentle stretching, swaying or dancing to your rhythm. As you move, imagine shedding the layers of societal expectations and stereotypes that may have burdened you. Embrace your unique identity and celebrate the diversity within you. Remember, being fully present with your feelings and emotions is the key. Welcome them without judgement, allowing all sensations to flow freely.

Humming

Place your hands over your heart centre and take a moment to connect with yourself deeply. Begin to hum softly, feeling the vibration resonate within your chest. Notice how the sound spreads throughout your body, cultivating a sense of harmony and unity. Allow the frequency of your sound to fill your heart and body with unconditional love. Release any self-doubt or insecurity, allowing your true essence to shine brightly.

Intuitive sounding

Allow yourself to make any sounds that naturally arise within you. All sounds are welcome, whether it's a sigh, a chuckle, or a cry. Trust that your inner voice knows exactly what it needs to express. Release any judgement or inhibition, and let your voice convey your emotions authentically. Keep sounding, and if you wish, create harmony with the sounds you make. Keep flowing with the rhythm of your inner voice.

Silence

Take a moment to savour the stillness that follows your sound. Allow yourself to immerse in the peace and tranquillity of the present moment. Notice any sensations or insights that arise within you as you embrace the power of silence.

Journaling prompts

- Reflect on your experience with breath, movement, humming, intuitive sounding and silence. How did each practice make you feel? Did any particular moments resonate with you?
- Explore the notion of reclaiming your voice as a person of mixed race or heritage. What does authentic self-expression mean to you?
- Consider any challenges or barriers you've encountered in owning your identity and voice. How can you navigate these obstacles and step into your power more confidently?
- Envision a future where you feel fully aligned with your true self. What actionable steps can you take to move towards that vision?
- Could you reflect on how you define yourself? Is being mixed race or mixed heritage the only way you define yourself, or are other aspects of your identity important to you? Take a moment to explore and acknowledge the various facets of your identity beyond racial or cultural background.

- Take your time to jot down your thoughts and feelings in your journal. Remember, this is a safe space for self-expression, and there are no right or wrong answers. Trust yourself and honour the journey you're embarking on.

EXERCISE 6: SPECTRUM OF IDENTITY

By Lydia Puricelli
(www.consciousculture.coach; @consciousculturecoach)

Understanding your Identity, Culture and Ethnicity

Identity: Reflect on the core elements that define your identity, what makes you, you? This includes your ethnicity and your culture. They don't always match like-for-like.

Culture: Think about the cultural origins you have, the customs, traditions, and behaviours that have influenced you, such as language, religion, spirituality, art, and social norms. Examples might include being Black, English, Queer, Goth, or identifying with a particular social class, such as Middle-class.

Ethnicity: Think about the ethnic groups you are grouped under. These may fall under your nationality, common linguistic, or ancestral background. List aspects of your ethnicity, such as your race, nationality, tribe, or clan.

There is no right or wrong for this exercise, do as you feel/see fit. The aspects of your ethnicity can be as large or as small as you like so you might have English and Caribbean heritage but also some Swedish, make them as large or as small as feels right to you and your unique lived experience. For example:

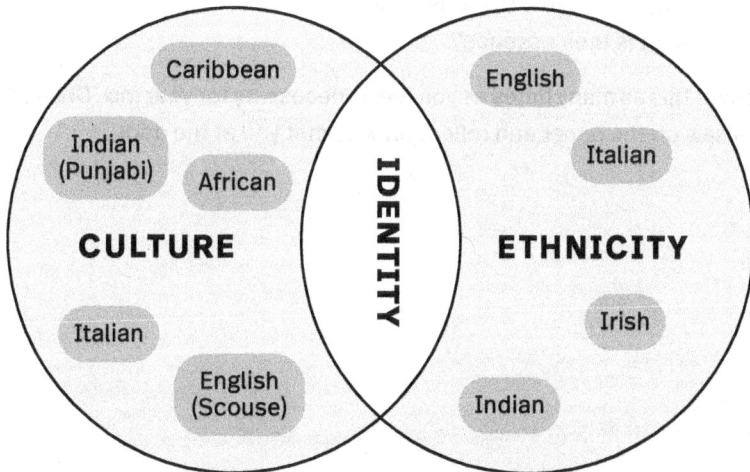

EXERCISE 7: YOUR CULTURAL PERSONALITIES EXERCISE

By Namalee Bolle
(namaleebolle.com; Instagram @mxdtherapist)

This exercise is based on an original visualisation meditation by the Centre for Counselling and Psychotherapy Education.

You will need a piece of paper and some pens.

- Take three deep breaths and make sure you are comfortable. Close your eyes when you feel ready to begin.
- Imagine you are in a beautiful open space outdoors in a landscape of your choice. You feel calm and peaceful.
- You see a house and you walk towards it.
- Inside the home are people, animals or mascots from your various cultural heritages.
- You go up to the front door and knock and wait to see who comes to the door.
- Notice how they greet you – what nationality are they?
- Which language are they speaking?
- What do they look like?
- What are they wearing?
- Are there any cultural symbols, colours or clothing?
- How do you feel towards them?
- What is their essence?

Repeat this as many times as you feel is necessary for your mix. Draw what you saw on the paper and reflect on who met you at the door.

EXERCISE 8: ANCESTRAL HERITAGE CONNECTION RITUAL

By Semra Haksever
(www.mamamooncandles.com; @mamamooncandles)

You will need:

- A white candle.
- 5ml oil of your choice (olive or almond is good).
- Any herbs, scents or flowers that are connected to your ancestral heritage: this could be herbs used in cooking or any plant that is native to a specific place, or an essential oil that invokes a memory.

1. Blend the herbs, flowers or scent with the oil.
2. Tip onto a plate and roll the candle in the blend.
3. Light the candle and say, 'Ancestors, I wish to connect.'
4. Clap your hands three times over the candle's flame.
5. You may choose to stare at the flame or close your eyes; imagine roots travelling down through your feet and travelling down to the centre of the earth.
6. As they travel down, tune into the power that walking on the earth before you were many ancestors walking on the same land.
7. Visualise your roots travelling through the earth to the place that your ancestors came from.
8. Feel a connection, visualise their life, their world, and as you do this zoom in and notice what feelings arise.
9. Listen out for messages or visions that may come up, or just simply enjoy the connection of your roots beneath the earth.
10. When you feel ready, open your eyes.
11. Blow the candle out and clap your hands three times again.
12. Always look out for intuitive signs afterwards, as messages may come through!

FURTHER RESOURCES

Poems (as seen in chapter epigraphs)
'Not Homogeneous' – Dr Isha Mckenzie-McVinga
'My Mother's White Daughter' – Ceilidh Ashcroft (as seen in *Middleground* Issue 3)
'BODYNOTABODY' – Hera Hong (as seen in *Middleground* Issue 2)
'Half-Stereotype' – Luke AG
'Half Normal' – Ramanique Ahluwalia
'Mixed Feelings' – Sophie-Kim Nguyễn
'+Trickster+' – Namalee Bolle
'Multicolored Heart' – Indira Midha
'Do You Have Superpower Problems?' – Kyley Winfield
'Namazonia' – Namalee Bolle

Further poems
'Half Caste' – John Agard
'I Come From' – Dean Atta
'Anatomy of My Mixed Body' – Katharine Threat

Film and TV
1000% ME: Growing Up Mixed
One Big Hapa Family
Mixed Marrow
Passing

Books, literature and publications
Middle Ground Magazine: A free literary and art magazine for mixed-race people
 and their identities, stories and voices. www.middlegroundmagazine.co.uk
www.tapecollective.co.uk
Mixed Bill of Rights by Dr Maria Primitiva Paz Root
The Half of It by Emma Slade Edmondson and Nicole Ocran
Not Quite White by Laila Woozeer
Mixed/Other by Natalie Morris
Biracial Britain by Remi Adekoya
Both Not Half by Jassa Ahluwalia
Boundless: Twenty Voices Celebrating Multicultural and Multiracial Identities edited by
 Esmee Williams and Rebecca Balcarcel
The Mixed Race Experience by Naomi and Natalie Evans
The Meaning of Mariah Carey by Mariah Carey
Mongrel by Hanako Footman
Raising Multiracial Children: Tools for Nurturing Identity in a Racialized World by Farzana
 Nayani
And... by Isabel Adonis
Mixed Feelings by Avan Jogia
The Racism of People Who Love You by Samira K. Mehta
High Yella: A Modern Family Memoir by Steve Majors
Born a Crime by Trevor Noah
The Vanishing Half by Britt Bennett
An Essential Guide to Caring for Afro and Mixed Race Children's Hair by Dr A. Rose

But What Will People Say? Navigating Mental Health, Identity, Love and Family Between Cultures by Sahaj Kaur Kohli

My Life in The Sunshine; Searching for My Father and Discovering My Family by Nabil Ayers

Kakigori Summer by Emily Itami

Children's books
I Am Whole by Shola Oz, illustrated by Shifa Annisa
Is That Your Mama? by Patrick Lawrence and Diane Ewen
Mixed Me by Taye Diggs, illustrated by Shane Evans
I Can Be All Three by Salima Alikhan and Noor Sofi
Where Are You From? by Yamile Saied Mendez and Jamie Kim
Our Skin: A First Conversation About Race by Megan Edison Jessica Ralli and Isabel Roxas
Curls by Ruth Forman
Hair Love by Matthew A. Cherry, illustrated by Vashti Harrison

Groups and courses
Mixed Race Meditation (A meditation space for multiracial individuals): https://www.mixedracemeditation.com
Mixed Asian Media: mixedasianmedia.com
The Mixed Space: themixedspace.com
BAATN Mosaic Group (for mixed therapists and practitioners only): www.baatn.org.uk
Free to Be Collective: freetobecollective.com
Rooted Global Village: rootedglobalvillage.com
Mixed in America: www.mixedinamerica.org

Collectives and platforms
@mixedmessagesnewsletter
@themixedgirlmeetup
@mixedpresent
@mixedrage
@mixedup.podcast
@Biraciallounge
@Mixedbloomroom
@drjennpsych
@militantlymixed
@mixedinamerica
@mosaicthelabel
@mixedracefaces
@beingbiracialpodcast
@multiracialmatters
@everydayracism_
@Iamblirish
@bodyjustice.therapist

Websites
Mixed Messages Substack: mixedmessages.substack.com
The Mixed Museum: mixedmuseum.org.uk

Mixed Race Studies: mixedracestudies.org
Mixed Marrow: mixedmarrow.org
Daren Banarsë's Unola: https://darenbanarse.com/unola
Mixed Messages with Sarah Doneghy: youtube.com/@mixedmessagesshow

Podcasts
Militantly Mixed
Mixed Up
Body Justice
Being Biracial
Sick and Sickening Podcast

Therapy + coaching + mental health
BAATN (Black and Asian Therapist Network): www.baatn.org.uk
Black Minds Matter UK: www.blackmindsmatteruk.com
South Asian Therapists: southasiantherapists.org
Muslim Counsellor & Psychotherapist Network: mcapn.co.uk
https://southasiantherapists.org
Radical Therapist Network: radicaltherapistnetwork.com
UKCP (UK Council for Psychotherapists): www.psychotherapy.org.uk
BACP (British Association of Counsellors and Psychotherapists): www.bacp.co.uk
Beat Eating Disorders: beateatingdisorders.org.uk
https://houseofself.co.uk
https://theselfspace.com
https:/ccpe.org.uk

Endnotes

Introduction

1   www.forbes.com/sites/earlcarr/2024/08/06/the-future-of-the-multi-cultural-biracial-and-multiracial-landscape
2   www.theguardian.com/society/2014/feb/23/mixed-race-children-mental-health
3   https://theface.com/life/mixed-race-identity-mental-health-black-minds-matter-imposter-syndrome-white-fragility

Chapter 1

1   https://www.reddit.com/r/mixedrace/ comments/17dgizi/ in_the_1990s_dr_maria_p_root_came_up_wi th_the
2   www.instagram.com/reel/C4UPrdOLnO_/?igsh=aTkyNDdwcDZoc3Nm
3   https://vm.tiktok.com/ZGeEer2xo
4   www.seventeen.com/celebrity/news/a38322/charli-xcx-responds-to-racist-comments-i-am-extremely-proud-of-my-indian-heritage
5   https://vm.tiktok.com/ZGeEeDsY3
6   www.google.co.uk/books/edition/Mixed_Other/6RDoDwAAQBAJ?hl=en&gb pv=1&dq=natalie+morris+author&printsec=frontcover

Chapter 2

1   www.dailymail.co.uk/news/article-7399617/Gold-Radio-bans-Melting-Pot-Blue-Mink-listener-complains-offensive-lyrics.html
2   www.cbsnews.com/video/w-kamau-bell-on-1000-me-growing-up-mixed-a-documentary-exploring-mixed-race-experience
3   https://x.com/bbcstories/status/1103620056213348353?s=46&t=LijlkIHUKX-Wq_2rDqRd56w
4   www.youtube.com/watch?v=fNfzvCc4Qpg
5   www.digitalspy.com/soaps/eastenders/a46788857/eastenders-anna-gina-knight-racism
6   www.bacp.co.uk/bacp-journals/therapy-today/2019/april-2019/between-black-and-white
7   https://theface.com/music/mabel-musician-pop-artist-interview-let-them-know

Chapter 3

1   www.amazon.co.uk/Mixed-Feelings-Avan-Jogia/dp/1449496210
2   https://vm.tiktok.com/ZGeKCFpJv
3   www.stylist.co.uk/entertainment/not-quite-white-laila-woozeer-mixed-race-identity-fetishisation/679428
4   www.theguardian.com/society/2020/oct/18/nhs-hospital-admissions-eating-disorders-rise-among-ethnic-minorities
5   https://www.beateatingdisorders.org.uk/your-stories/black-history-month-at-beat
6   www.theguardian.com/commentisfree/2021/apr/08/why-celebrating-mixed-race-beauty-has-its-problematic-side
7   https://mixedmessages.substack.com/p/albert-magashi-mixed-race-interview
8   https://theface.com/music/fka-twigs-interview-michaela-coel-i-may-destroy-you-pa-salieu-headie-one

Chapter 4

1   www.shsoutherner.net/blogs/73daysletters/2016/12/10/your-silence-will-not-protect-you-healing-with-audre-lorde
2   https://www.youtube.com/watch? v=xJrg41b5RFM

Chapter 5

1   https://people.com/lenny-kravitz-black-man-whoembraces-his-full-heritage-exclusive-8557643
2   www.theguardian.com/commentisfree/2022/aug/30/mixed-person-language-vocabulary
3   www.reddit.com/r/mixedrace/comments/qlw3py/do_you_describe_your_mix_with_a
4   www.apa.org/pubs/videos/4310742-rights.pdf
5   https://www.theguardian.com/music/2013/oct/19/eartha-kitt-suffered-over-identity
6   https://www.bbc.co.uk/culture/article/20250109-eartha-kitt-from-extreme-povertyto-stardom
7   www.vfdalston.com/exhibitions/2023/11/28/mixed-rage-unapologetically-other
8   www.theaustralian.com.au/subscribe/news/1/?sourceCode=TAWEB_WRE170_a_GGL&dest=https%3A%2F%2Fwww.theaustralian.com.au%2Fsport%2Folympics%2Fburning-issue-how-japanese-is-naomi-osaka%2Fnews-story%2F0795aa70964e46c1ea8a7b23a79f3c58&memtype=anonymous&mode=premium&v21=HIGH-Segment-1-SCORE&V21spcbehaviour=append
9   www.standard.co.uk/comment/mixed-race-identity-toxic-debate-b1154047.html

Chapter 6

1   www.youtube.com/watch?v=aGOqBgqWcr8
2   www.marieclaire.co.uk/opinion/Kamala-Harris-Black-heritage-Trump
3   www.bbc.co.uk/news/articles/c2501n5rvvno
4   www.youtube.com/watch?v=zs5dI4XH63o
5   https://www.migrationmuseum.org/census-reveals-new-chapter-in-story-of-mixed-race-britain
6   https://www.google.co.uk/books/edition/Depth_Psychology_Meditations_in_the_Fiel/md51CQAAQBAJ?hl=en&gbpv=1&dq=jungian+analyst+hillman+tension+of+the+opposites&pg=PA236&prints ec=frontcover

7   www.rootedglobalvillage.com/belonging-reg-europe
8   https://mixedmessages.substack.com/p/poppy-ajudha-regardless-of-how-people
9   https://www.mixedinamerica.org
10 https://theface.com/music/fka-twigs-interview-michaela-coel-i-may-destroy-you-pa-salieu-headie-one
11 https://psycnet.apa.org/record/2011-12742-006
12 www.psychiatry.org/getmedia/bac9c998-5b2d-4ffa-ace9-d35844b8475a/Mental-Health-Facts-for-Diverse-Populations.pdf
13 http://mixedmarrow.org/aboutus/sample-page
14 https://mixedmessages.substack.com/p/poppy-ajudha-regardless-of-how-people
15 www.facebook.com/BBCOne/videos/tan-france-talks-colourism-on-the-cards-bbc/408003947794000
16 www.baatn.org.uk
17 www.youtube.com/watch?v=qlvM2k216Os

Chapter 7

1   www.nationalelfservice.net/populations-and-settings/black-and-minority-ethnic/multiracial-people-mental-health
2   https://pih.org.uk/front-page/mixed-race-suicide-risk
3   www.ft.com/content/563bd9fd-e05f-4e38-9334-897e2e325f7d
4   www.eonline.com/news/1399947/miss-usa-2019-cheslie-kryst-details-mental-health-struggles-in-posthumous-memoir
5   www.amazon.co.uk/Biracial-Britain-What-Means-Mixed/dp/1472133455
6   www.youtube.com/watch?v=VxYx2dDIXd4
7   https://x.com/adam_nimoy/status/1775233743873048806?s=46&t=RZg_0n2keyWYu_35f1rsRA

Chapter 10

1   https://www.theguardian.com/culture/article/2024/jun/30/we-now-feel-proud-tobe-mixed-the-blessings-and-biases-of-beingbiracial
2   https://genius.com/4638051/X-ray-spex-identity/When-you-look-in-the-mirror-do-you-see-yourself-do-you-see-yourself-on-the-tv-screen
3   www.dazeddigital.com/film-tv/article/52112/1/poly-styrene-i-am-cliche-punk-seven-songs-life-music-celeste-bell-interview
4   https://www.youtube.com/watch?v=rKCIZf8qDLA
5   https://anderson-review.ucla.edu/multiracial
6   https://vm.tiktok.com/ZGeKTky8g
7   www.psychologytoday.com/gb/articles/201905/the-biracial-advantage
8   www.whitecube.com/artists/isamu-noguchi
9   http://mixedracestudies.org
10 www.bbc.co.uk/programmes/p097hf2p
11 www.amazon.co.uk/Boundless-Celebrating-Multicultural-Multiracial-Identities/dp/1335428615
12 www.noguchi.org/wp-content/uploads/2019/08/Isamu-Noguchi-I-Become-A-Nisei-The-Noguchi-Museum.pdf
13 www.mixedremixed.org/pains-joys-mixed-race
14 www.psychologytoday.com/gb/blog/living-between-worlds/201706/biracial-dating-in-a-monoracial-culture
15 www.youtube.com/watch?v=rOztzgQiV1o

16   https://store.hbr.org/product/hbr-s-10-must-reads-on-managing-across-cultures-with-featured-article-cultural-intelligence-by-p-christopher-earley-and-elaine-mosakowski/10016?srsltid=AfmBOoqiosAPt1gPSabclmdXDJh EL7-olssQtddhdrvI-zdWaPEk7836

Chapter 11

1   www.forbes.com/2010/02/01/immigration-multiracial-superpower-opinions-columnists-joel-kotkin.html
2   https://www.bbc.co.uk/news/resources/idt-sh/celebrating_our_mixed_race_identity
3   www.bbc.co.uk/news/resources/idt-sh/celebrating_our_mixed_race_identity
4   www.amnesty.org.uk/files/2019-01/I%20Come%20From%20by%20Dean%20 Atta.pdf?KodcWa_ba959rPZHtfw5WHIjiLz6okNC=
5   https://jwa.org/blog/how-celebrity-chef-helpedme-connect-my-mixed-heritage
6   @afrogermangirl
7   www.ted.com/talks/emma_slade_edmondson_the_fabric_of_life?subtitle=en